DREK!

The Real Yiddish You Should Be So Lucky to Learn

BULVON
A man who's built like an ox
(and acts like one, too).

GAY IN DRERD
Drop dead
(literally, "go into the ground").

TUKHES LECHER
A butt kisser.

ZAFTIG
A plump, appealing woman
(literally, "juicy").

PUPIK
Belly button.

FREG NIT
Don't ask.

DREK!
The REAL Yiddish Your Bubbeh Never Taught You

Yetta Emmes

Illustrations by Kim Wilson Brandt

A PLUME BOOK

PLUME
Published by the Penguin Group
Penguin Putnam Inc., 375 Hudson Street,
New York, New York 10014, U.S.A.
Penguin Books Ltd, 27 Wrights Lane,
London W8 5TZ, England
Penguin Books Australia Ltd, Ringwood,
Victoria, Australia
Penguin Books Canada Ltd, 10 Alcorn Avenue,
Toronto, Ontario, Canada M4V 3B2
Penguin Books (N.Z.) Ltd, 182–190 Wairau Road,
Auckland 10, New Zealand

Penguin Books Ltd, Registered Offices:
Harmondsworth, Middlesex, England

First published by Plume, an imprint of Dutton NAL,
a member of Penguin Putnam Inc.

First Printing, December, 1998
10   9

 REGISTERED TRADEMARK—MARCA REGISTRADA

LIBRARY OF CONGRESS CATALOGING-IN-PUBLICATION DATA:

Emmes, Yetta.
   Drek! : the real Yiddish your bubbeh never taught you / Yetta Emmes : illustrations by Kim
Wilson Brandt.
      p.   cm.
   ISBN 0-452-27899-6
   1. Yiddish language—Idioms.   2. Yiddish language—Spoken Yiddish.   3. Yiddish language—
Slang.   4. Yiddish language—Terms and phrases.
I. Title
PJ5118.E66   1998
439'.183421—dc21   98-27347
                                                                                                     CIP

Printed in the United States of America
Set in Janson
Designed by Leonard Telesca

BOOKS ARE AVAILABLE AT QUANTITY DISCOUNTS WHEN USED TO PROMOTE PRODUCTS OR SERVICES.
FOR INFORMATION PLEASE WRITE TO PREMIUM MARKETING DIVISION, PENGUIN PUTNAM INC., 375
HUDSON STREET, NEW YORK, NEW YORK 10014.

Contents

Contents

Contents

Introduction

When Mark Twain said, "Reports of my death are greatly exaggerated," he could have been speaking for Yiddish. It's been called a dying language for a hundred years and yet you won't have to look very hard to find Yiddish speakers in almost all parts of the world—millions of them. It is truly an international language. In New York, London, Paris, Buenos Aires, Jerusalem, and countless other locales you'll hear Yiddish folk chattering away in their ancient tongue, doing business, telling jokes, talking philosophy, gossiping, counseling their children and, of course, arguing.

And you'll find Yiddish-language departments in universities throughout the United States, and Yiddish study classes in synagogues and community centers. And you can see Yiddish theater companies performing old and new plays for eager audiences in New York and Miami, and then, like their famous thespian forerunners (from Jacob Adler to Molly Picon), taking their troupes on international tours.

You'll also encounter countless Yiddish expressions that have crept into English and other languages. Call someone a *shmuck*, a *nudnik*, a *gonif*, or a *kibbitzer*, you're speaking Yiddish.

Of course, a language with such chutzpah isn't about to fold up and die. Ah, but if you are a goy or an "assimilated Jew," you may not know what *chutzpah* means. You may not even know what *goy* means. Well, here's your first Yiddish lesson. A *goy* is anyone who is not Jewish, be it a guy goy (a *shaygetz*) or a girl goy (a *shikseh*), and sometimes nonobservant Jews are also referred to (unflatteringly) as *goys*, as in "You're such a goy."

Returning to *chutzpah*, in today's American vernacular, it might be translated as "having balls." When you compliment someone for his chutzpah, you're saying he is daring, that he'll stand up to the big guy (King David had chutzpah; Barbara Walters has chutzpah—note that women can have balls too). But you can also criticize someone for his chutzpah ("He has *such* chutzpah"). Then you're saying he goes too far, he has unmitigated gall, he's in your face. He's beyond nervy; he's got some nerve.

Whether you are goy or Jew, you probably do know a host of Yiddish words that have made their way into every arena of modern life, from show business to law. For example, a recent law journal noted that since 1980 the word *chutzpah* has appeared in judicial decisions 101 times (maybe judges have more chutzpah these days). And the word *shmuck* appeared fifty-nine times in reference to a litigant (as in, "My client admits he was a shmuck for doing that, but Your Honor . . ."); it even appeared once in a case before the Supreme Court.

So, where did this vibrant language begin? Scholars trace its origins back a thousand years to the tenth century, when Jews were chased from northern France (so what else is new?) and settled in German cities along the Rhine. By the fifteenth century Yiddish had evolved into a distinct language, similar to German but with its own pronunciation and linguistic characteristics. It's not surprising that speakers of German and Yiddish can often understand each other to some degree.

Even though many of its words derive from Hebrew and Aramaic, and though it is written in the Hebrew alphabet,

Yiddish is a European language—the *mameh loshen* (or mother tongue) of the Ashkenazim, the Jews of Europe. It was never spoken by the Sephardic Jews of Spain and Portugal, nor by their descendants who migrated to Syria, Egypt, and other Middle Eastern communities after they were kicked out of Spain by Queen Isabella in 1492 (a very bad year for both Jews and Native Americans).

Like any living language, Yiddish continued to evolve over the centuries. As the Jews migrated into the various countries of Eastern Europe, Yiddish was enriched by words and phrases derived from the languages of the countries where they settled, such as Poland, Russia, Hungary, and Romania. In turn, Yiddish evolved into a number of different dialects, such as Litvak (from Lithuania) and Galiciana (from Galicia, which spanned parts of Poland and the Ukraine).

Yiddish is the language of a culture, not of a country (Hebrew is the official language of Israel, and, of course, the language of the Jewish religion). Yiddish was heard in the ghettos and shtetls, and in the many other large and small Jewish communities spread across Central and Eastern Europe. But, as we all know too well, during the past hundred years the Jews fled those communities in two massive waves. Around the turn of the century, they left Czarist Russia (think *Fiddler on the Roof*, only worse), and during the Nazi era, those who could fled from just about everywhere else in Europe. Jews were scattered all over the world from Shanghai and Caracas to Johannesburg and Montreal. But for the most part the European Jewish culture resettled in the United States, with New York City its unofficial capital.

Soon Yiddish became the language of Delancey Street and the Lower East Side, and Williamsburg and Ocean Parkway and the Grand Concourse and the garment center in Midtown Manhattan. In the summers you could hear it in the Catskills, and in the winters in Miami Beach. Soon you could hear it on Maxwell Street in Chicago, in the Dorchester section of

Boston, and the Fairfax section of Los Angeles. You could even hear it in Hollywood if you listened closely (in the executive offices, not on the screen). Nowadays you'll hear Yiddish in cities and suburbs all across America; from Atlanta, Georgia, to Lakewood, New Jersey, to Monsey, New York.

Although Yiddish is still very much alive, it may be harder today to learn many of the colorful words and phrases that were an intrinsic part of its vocabulary when it was the daily language of workingmen cutting fabrics in clothing factories, or women gossiping in front of tenements, or vaudeville comics performing their bawdy skits at Minsky's Burlesque.

Yiddish "street" slang may not make it into the curriculum of the courses taught in the synagogue or the Workmen's Circle. Nor is it likely to be taught by parents and *bubbehs* and *zaydas* (*grandmothers* and *grandfathers* to the uninitiated) who want to pass on the language to their little Rachels and Isaacs.

That's where this book will come in handy. In the following pages you'll find many of those everyday terms—the colorful and the *off*-color—that don't always appear in phrase books and dictionaries. To you, the reader, we say "*Zets zich avek* [sit down and enjoy]." And to Yiddish, the language of a culture that has enriched human civilization as much as any other, we say: "May you live at least another thousand years."

A Note on Pronunciation and Spelling

As George and Ira Gershwin might have said (or sung), "You say *maydle* and I say *mydle*; you say *zayda* and I say *zyda*. . . ." In other words, how Yiddish speakers pronounce the words for *girl*, *grandfather*, and many others depends on their regional accent. Like other languages, Yiddish comes in a number of different dialects. Here, I'll use the form that is considered "standard" in some major texts on Yiddish pronunciation, although in a living language there really is no standard pronunciation and, frankly, the texts often differ from each other.

Also, scholars differ on the best way to spell Yiddish words in English (some write *shlemiel*, others write *schlemiehl*). Here, I've tried to spell words in the least complicated way and added a pronunciation aid that provides both sound and stress, as in *gefilte* (geh-FIL-teh) fish. By the way, if your child asks you what kind of bait to use to catch a gefilte fish, you'll know you're not passing on key elements of the Jewish heritage.

Sometimes Yiddish conversation sounds like people clearing their throats, which brings up the fact that there are a few sounds in Yiddish that may give some English speakers difficulty. For example, the *ch* in *chutzpah* (CHUTZ-pah) is one of those throat-clearing sounds, pronounced as a soft *k* (but hit a bit further back on the palate than our standard plosive *k*). To make life easier for themselves, some English speakers turn the *ch* into an *h* and say *hutzpah*. In the pronunciation guide that accompanies each word in this book, you'll usually find this sound indicated by the letters *kh*, as in the word *yakhneh*. But sometimes you'll find a *ch*, as in *chutzpah* and *ich* (which means *I*). These are words that many readers will have seen written with a *ch*, so to avoid confusion it seemed best to keep the *ch*.

The *r* sound, as in the word *rebbe* (REH-beh), is another troubling one for American speakers. Depending on dialect, it can be guttural (make a gargle sound from the back of your throat) or trilled (vibrate your tongue against your upper palate close to where it meets your teeth).

I
People: The Good, The Bad, and The Ugly

It always happens. You're discussing someone with a friend whose first language is Yiddish, and he throws in a Yiddish word to describe that person. You'll ask what the word means, and he'll struggle to give you a definition, often having to use a whole sentence to convey the essence and spirit of that one perfect word. Sometimes he'll throw his hands up and exclaim, "It can't be translated!"

The fact is that Yiddish has produced a lot of great words that capture, succinctly and precisely, the fine details of human character, as well as the great diversity of human characters. Take *mensch*, a word that has crept into common English usage. Literally, it means *person* or *human being*. But it implies so much more: A mensch is upright and sensible; he meets his obligations, keeps his head, and treats others fairly; he'll make a good business partner and a good husband. That's packing a lot into one word, and you won't find an English term that says it quite as well (which is why it is often used in English today). And it's used for women as well as men.

One special category of descriptive terms will be saved for

its own chapter. These are the *sh* words—words beginning with the *sh* sound. There are surprisingly many of them and most refer to one or another kind of fool or misfit. More on these in the next chapter, but for now here is a rich collection of savory Yiddish terms for describing the most common human characteristics—*the good, the bad, and the ugly.*

The Good

Balehbusteh *(ba-leh-BUST-eh)*—a top-notch homemaker. Often used as a compliment to a recent bride who has made her new home cozy and efficient ("She's become such a *balehbusteh*").

Gezinteh *(geh-ZIN-teh*)*—a healthy, robust person; commonly used to refer to a he-man—or a well-endowed woman.

Gezunt vi a ferd *(geh-ZUNT vee ah FERD)*—as strong (literally, healthy) as a horse.

Ying mit bainer *(YING mit BAY-nehr)*—literally, a boy with sturdy bones; a strong and sturdy young man; a powerhouse.

Shtarker *(SHTARK-er)*—a strong person. When you need your piano moved, it's useful to have a friend who is a *shtarker*.

Shtark vi a ferd *(SHTARK vee a FERD)*—as strong as a horse.

Lantzman *(LONTZ-mon)*—a fellow countryman; someone who grew up in the same city or shtetl; metaphorically, a kindred spirit or soul mate; kind of like a homeboy.

Haymisheh *(HAY-mish-eh)*—someone who is warm and welcoming; a homey, unaffected person, with whom one is comfortable.

Bubeleh *(BUB-eh-leh)*—literally, little grandmother. Used as a term of endearment for children. It has also become a syn-

---

*The *g* is always hard in Yiddish, no matter what vowel follows it. *Ge* in *gez-inteh* is pronounced like *gue* in *guess*.

Drek!

onym for *dear* and *honey*, and one will even hear it used among men as a lighthearted expression of fondness or conciliation (as in, "Yes, *bubeleh*, the check really *is* in the mail.").

Balebatish *(BAL-eh-BAT-ish)*—a fine person; responsible and honorable; someone you can count on.

Khochem *(KHOH-khem)* or **Khochema** *(fem.)*—a wise or brilliant person. The ultimate tribute to a scholar. A Mac-Arthur Award winner would be called a *khochem* or *khochema*.

Maven *(MAY-vin)*—an expert, a connoisseur; anyone who is an authority on a subject. Frank Perdue is a chicken *maven* (but only for non-kosher chickens).

Mensch *(mentsh)*—a good person, worthy of respect; a human being with feelings for others and a sense of humanity. The opposite of a *schmuck*.

Gooteh neshumeh *(GOOT-eh nuh-SHOOM-eh)*—*neshumeh* means soul. *A gooteh neshumeh* is a good soul; a person who can't hate.

Haimisheh mensch *(HAME-ish-eh MENTSH)*—a warm person who makes you feel comfortable; someone you feel at home with (from the word *haim*, meaning home).

A lebedickeh mensch *(a LEB-eh-DICK-eh MENTSH)*—a lively, spirited person.

Aidel *(AY-del)*—genteel, cultured, modest.

Feinshmeker *(FINE-shmek-er)*—a person with fine taste; elite, highfalutin.

Farbrenter *(far-BRENT-er)*—someone who "burns" with enthusiasm or is impulsive; a big fan.

Khaver *(KHA-ver)*—male friend.

Khaverteh *(KHA-ver-teh)*—female friend.

Yiddisher kop *(YID-ish-er KUP)*—literally, a Jewish head. Someone smart, who grasps things quickly.

Kibbitzer *(KIB-itz-er)*—someone who kibbitzes; a jokester, a teaser or a person who butts into other people's business.

Kuntzenmakher *(KOONTZ-in-MAKH-er)*—a trickster, a magician.

Parshoin *(PAR-shoyn)*—a he-man or hero. Moshe Dayan was a *parshoin*.

Zaftig *(ZAF-tig)*—literally, juicy. Commonly used to refer to a plump, appealing woman—a woman who is good to squeeze and usually well-stacked, like Bette Midler or Dolly Parton.

Yakhsen *(YAKH-sen)*—a distinguished person of aristocratic lineage.

Molodyets *(mol-OD-yets)*—a clever fellow.

On a Miami Beach street, Leibgold, walking his Great Dane, bumped into his childhood friend and partner in mischief, Farkus, who was walking his Chihuahua. Overjoyed, Leibgold implored his old buddy to join him for lunch in a nearby restaurant.

"But we have dogs," said Farkus.

Leibgold winked. "Follow me and do what I do."

As they entered the fancy restaurant, the maître d' stopped Leibgold.

"You cannot come in here with that dog," he said.

"But it's my Seeing Eye dog," Leibgold replied.

"I'm so sorry, sir. The hostess will show you to a table."

As Farkus stepped forward, the maître d' hopped in front of him. "Sir, you can't come in here with that dog."

Farkus, following Leibgold's instructions, replied, "It's my Seeing Eye dog."

Smirking, the maître d' asked, "That Chihuahua is a Seeing Eye dog?"

Drek!

With a startled look on his face, Farkus, ever the *molodyets*, replied, "They gave me a Chihuahua?"

The Bad

Geshtruft *(geh-SHTRUFT)*—cursed, accursed; someone born unlucky.

Bondit *(bon-DEET)*—a bandit. Can be used admiringly to describe someone as clever who is good at getting away with things or beating the system; a clever rascal. Also used affectionately for a clever child.

Balmalokheh *(bal-mal-OH-kheh)*—an expert, as in "As a tailor, he's a *balmalokheh*."

Groisser sheeser *(GROY-ser SHEE-ser)*—a big shot.

Pisk-Malokheh *(PISK MAL-oh-kheh)*—a big talker who does little. A *pisk-malokheh* is an expert only with his mouth (or *pisk*). Someone who talks the talk but doesn't walk the walk.

Khazer *(KHAZ-ehr)*—literally, a pig. Commonly, a greedy person; someone who takes more than his or her share. Someone who eats too much.

Kokhlefel *(KOHKH-lefel)*—literally, a cooking ladle. Someone who stirs up trouble by mixing in everyone's business. A gossip.

Yenta *(YEN-teh)*—a busybody, a gossip. (Common now in English.)

Farshtinkener *(far-SHTINK-en-er)*—a disgusting, smelly person. Also someone with a stinky character who is selfish and insincere.

Shtik drek *(shtik DREK)*—literally, a piece of shit; an odious person; a shithead.

Makhashaifeh *(makh-ah-SHAYF-eh)*—a witch; a mean woman. In jokes, often associated with mothers-in-law.

Hondler *(HOND-ler)*—someone who bargains or is always looking for an angle; the *hondler* never gives without getting.

Balehbos *(bal-eh-BOSS)*—the big boss; the head of the family or the business. Meyer Lansky was a *balehbos*.

Khokhem attick *(KHOKH-em AT-tik)*—a smart aleck or wise guy.

Nukhshlepper *(NOKH-shlep-per)*—a tagalong, a hanger-on who is not wanted.

Parekh *(PAR-ekh)*—a lowlife; a bad man.

Untervelt mensch *(UN-ter-velt MENTSH)*—a person from the underworld; a racketeer or gangster.

Koketkeh *(ko-KET-keh)*—coquette, flirt, a tease.

Shkapeh *(SHKAP-eh)*—a hag; also cheap or worthless object.

Cam vos er crekht *(cam vos air CREKHT)*—literally, He's barely able to creep; a decrepit person.

Groisser gornicht *(GROY-ser GOR-nicht)*—a big nothing; a blowhard.

Yatehbedam *(ya-teh-BEH-dahm)*—a blusterer. Someone who utters empty threats.

Golem *(GOL-em)*—a zombie; a dull, graceless oaf.

Klipeh *(KLIP-eh)*—a shrew or fiendish woman (a female demon).

A niderriktikeh kerl *(a NID-er-RIK-tik-eh KERL)*—a good-for-nothing; a low-down scoundrel; a lowlife.

Oysvorf *(OYS-vorf)*—an outcast, a pariah. Literally, a throwaway.

Yungatsh *(YUNG-atsh)*—a scamp or street urchin.

7

Gehakteh tzores *(geh-HAKH-teh TZOR-es)*—utter misery.

Baizeh khaieh *(BAYZ-eh KHA-yeh)*—literally, an angry animal. A person so vicious as to be inhuman; to act like a crazed animal.

Nishtgudnik *(nisht-GUD-nik)*—a no-goodnik; a bad person.

Kolboynik *(kol-BOY-nik)*—a know-it-all.

Yakhneh *(YAKH-neh)*—a meddling, loudmouthed, uncouth woman. (Often married to a *krekhtzer*.)

Paskudnik *(pas-KUD-nik)*—a nasty, deceiving lowlife, as in "Saddam Hussein is a *paskudnik*."

Gonif *(GON-if)*—a thief, a swindler, a chiseler. Put a gonif and a nebbish together and—oy vay!

> At Rubin's trial for pickpocketing, the judge declared, "Mr. Rubin, you are a *gonif* and must pay a fine of one hundred dollars."
> Rubin's lawyer stepped forward and said, "Your Honor, my client doesn't have a hundred dollars, but if you give him a few minutes in the crowd . . ."

The Ugly

Karger *(KAR-ger)*—a cheapskate, a miser, a skinflint, a tightwad—a good word for the guy who never comes to the UJA fund-raiser.

Parshiveh *(PAR-shiv-eh)*—mean, cheap.

Balagoleh *(bah-la-GOH-leh)*—a vulgar, menial person.

Bulvon *(BULL-von)*—a man built like an ox who also thinks like an ox; strong but also dumb and crude.

Klutz *(klutz)*—a clumsy person; graceless. A bungler, a clod. A Jerry Lewis type.

Drek!

Vilde mensch *(VIL-deh mentsh)*—a wild person; deranged; feral. Think of almost any hard-rock singer.

Nudnik *(NUD-nik)*—a pest, a nuisance, a nudge, a nag. Someone who is persistent to the point of annoyance. Most children.

Nishtikeit *(NISH-teh-kite)*—a nobody.

Nebbish *(NEB-ish)*—a nobody; a sad sack; inept, innocuous, ineffectual. Woody Allen made a career out of playing a *nebbish*.

Nebekh *(NEB-ekh)*—a nothing. A *nebekh* is like a nebbish, only more pitiful. *Nebekh* can also be used to express sympathy: "He got sick, the poor *nebekh*."

Kalehkeh *(KAL-eh-keh)*—a misfit, a maladroit. The *kalehkeh* is an expert at doing things poorly. Also a cripple.

Behaimeh *(buh-HAY-meh)*—a dumb animal. A stupid, dull person. Someone with the brains of a cow. A *behaimeh* knows how to make a touchdown, but don't ask him how to spell it.

Grober *(GRO-ber)*—a coarse, vulgar, uncouth person. Use it for the person who picks his teeth or his nose.

Kunyehlemel *(kun-yee-LEM-el)*—a naive, gullible man. Based on a character in a story by Avram Goldfaden.

Knocker *(K-NOCK-er)*—a big shot or show-off.

Prosteh mensch *(PROS-teh mentsh)*—worse than a *grober*; more of a lowlife.

Tummler *(TOOM-ler)*—an agitator; someone who stirs up things or demands everyone's attention.

Pisher *(PISH-er)*—a bed wetter; also refers to an inexperienced, unseasoned person, someone "wet behind the ears"; a squirt who can't be trusted with adult tasks (but thinks he can): "Who does he think he is?—the little *pisher*."

9

Luftmensch *(LOOFT-mentsh)*—a dreamer whose schemes lack substance (they are like the air); an unrealistic optimist with his head in the clouds; a poetic but impractical soul. Someone not to loan money to.

Ongehblozzen *(ON-geh-bloyz-en)*—a conceited, haughty person; puffed up with pride, full of himself.

Meeskeit *(MEES-kite)*—an ugly person. How ugly? So ugly it hurts the eyes.

Amorets *(ahm-OR-etz)*—an ignoramus, a boor; also, a peasant.

Orehman *(OR-eh-mon)*—poor man. In the old country it was said that when a poor farmer eats a chicken, one of them is sick.

Alter cocker *(AL-ter KOCK-er)*—literally, an old defecator. An old fogy (whose memory and bowels ain't what they used to be).

It was the alter cocker's birthday and his friends sent him a gorgeous prostitute as a surprise gift. When he opened the door, the sexy woman in the doorway leaned in and whispered, "I'm here for super sex." The old man thought for a minute, then replied, "Thank you. I'll have the soup."

Farbissener *(far-BISS-in-er)*—a sourpuss; a bitter person. Someone who always looks as if he has a bad taste in his mouth.

Makher *(MAKH-er)*—a big shot, mogul, or boss. Someone with the power to make things happen. Also used derisively for someone who has arrogated power to himself: "He thinks he's a *makher*."

Dumkop *(DOOM-kup)*—a dumbbell.

Goldfarb was stopped as he tried to enter the synagogue on Yom Kippur.

"You don't have a ticket," said the usher.

"I need to go in for just a minute. I have to give a message to Lipsky."

"Just for a minute," the *dumkop* replied, "but don't let me catch you praying."

Altvarg (*ALT-varg*)—a decrepit person, long past his prime.

Umshteller (*UM-shtel-er*)—a braggart, a show-off, an all-around know-it-all.

Izzy, the *umshteller*, applied for a job as a logger and was asked if he had any experience chopping down trees.

"I chopped down thousands of trees in the Sahara Forest," he replied.

"Don't you mean the Sahara Desert?" asked the foreman.

Izzy gave him a big smile. "Now it's a desert."

Tamavateh (*tam-eh-VAT-eh*)—a naive or simpleminded person.

Bulbenik (*bull-BEN-ik*)—an inept, clumsy person who has a way of ruining everything.

Alter bokher (*AL-ter BOOKH-er*)—bachelor; literally, an old schoolboy.

Alteh moid (*AL-teh MOYD*)—a spinster, an old maid.

Eighty-year-old Rosie burst into the men's shower room of the old-age home, and holding her fist out announced, "Anyone who guesses what's in my hand can have sex with me."

"An elephant," shouted a naked man in the corner.

"Close enough!" replied Rosie.

Funfer *(FUN-fer)*—someone who can't talk straight; a double-talker.

Meshuggener *(meh-SHOOG-en-er)*—a crazy person.

Draykop *(DRAY-kup)*—someone who confuses you, often to take advantage of you; a con artist or fast-talker (someone who "turns your head").

Umglicklekher *(UM-glick-lekh-er)*—an unlucky person; a born loser for whom nothing turns out well.

Laidik gayer *(LAY-dick GAY-er)*—idler, a loafer; someone with nothing in his pockets.

Kapsten *(KAP-sten)*—a pauper; someone below the poverty level.

Poyer *(POY-er)*—a peasant.

Greener *(GRIN-ner)*—a newcomer, a greenhorn; used by immigrant Jews to refer to someone not yet Americanized.

> Overheard in a science class for recent immigrants:
> Teacher: Today we will learn about the vacuum of outer space.
> Greener: Excuse me, teacher, would you define *vacuum*?
> Teacher: It's a void.
> Greener: I know it's a *void*, but vat das it mean?

Yold *(yold)*—a chump, a hick, a yokel; someone easily duped.

Kvetcher *(KVETCH-er)*—from *kvetch*, to squeeze; commonly refers to a complainer or griper. Nothing is ever good enough for the *kvetch*. Rodney Dangerfield is the King of *Kvetchers*.

Kvitcher *(KVITCH-er)*—someone who yelps or squeals. One "*gives a kvitch.*"

Krekhtzer *(KREKH-tzer)*—a complainer or fusser; someone who grunts and groans; a crank; a hypochondriac. If a man gives a woman a *kvetch*, she might, if she is surprised, give a *kvitch* and if she is angry, she will *krekhtz* about it all day long.

Goy Words

In the traditional world of the Jew, a sharp distinction was made between "us" and "them"; that is, between Jew and non-Jew (or gentile). The Yiddish word for gentile is *goy*, and when *goy* is connected to other words, the compound term describes one or another non-Jewish traits or characteristics. Here are a few common *goy* terms.

Shaygetz *(SHAY-getz)*—non-Jewish boy or man.

Shikseh *(SHICK-seh)*—non-Jewish girl or woman.

Goy *(masc.)*, **goyeh** *(fem.)*, **goyim** *(pl.)*—any gentile. Someone who buys retail.

Goyisher nokhes *(GOY-ish-er NOKH-es)*—pleasure from doing something traditionally un-Jewish, like hang gliding, auto racing, or entering a rural beer drinking contest.

Goyisher kop *(GOY-ish-er KUP)*—used derisively to refer to someone stupid or dim-witted.

Shabbes goy *(SHAH-bis GOY)*—literally, a gentile doing work (like turning lights on, igniting the stove) for Orthodox Jews on the Sabbath, when all work is prohibited. Also used to refer to someone doing another's dirty work.

Shtik goy *(shtick goy)*—an irreligious Jew.

II
The <u>Sh</u> Words: For Fools, Misfits, and Other Dysfunctional Types

Eskimos have a lot of words for different kinds of snow, and by God they need them. Jews, on the other hand, have an abundance of words to describe the many forms of human foolishness. And, interestingly, many of these words begin with the sound *sh* (which some scholars say derives from the German word *schlimm*, meaning bad). Why, you may wonder, does Yiddish make such fine distinctions between different types of fools? Maybe such fine shades of meaning make it easier to learn from others' mistakes. Or maybe it just makes for funnier stories. Whatever the reason, I'm sure you've all encountered your fair share of the following:

Shlemiel *(shleh-MEAL)*—a foolish person, a simpleton, a dolt, a bungler; a nincompoop who would not only buy the Brooklyn Bridge but offer to resell it, two for the price of one.

Shlemazel *(shleh-MAH-zel)*—a born loser, someone for whom nothing seems to go right or turn out well. When the shlemiel spills his soup, it always lands on the shlemazel.

A *shlemazel* and a *shlemiel* were walking home from the supermarket, bags filled with supplies, when a big wad of bird doo plopped on the *shlemazel*'s shoulder. He pouted and asked his companion if he had any toilet paper in his bags. The *shlemiel* said, "What difference would it make? That bird must be five miles away by now."

Shmegegee *(shmeh-GEH-gee)*—like a *shlemiel* but even less important; a drip, a jerk, a nobody.

Mr. Katz came home early and discovered his wife having sex with a stranger.
"What are you doing?" shouted the irate husband.
"See," the wife said to the man in bed with her. "I told you he was a *shmegegee*."

Shmendrick *(SHMEN-drick)*—from the name of a character in an operetta by Avram Goldfaden; a kind of *shlemiel*, but feeble and spineless; a pip-squeak, a weakling, a simpleton; also used by women to refer to a small penis.

Shmuck *(shmuck)*—one can pity a *shlemiel* and a *shlemazel*, but a *shmuck* is mean-spirited as well as stupid; an asshole (metaphorically, not literally), a prick. Also literally refers to a penis, which may derive from its basic meaning, an ornament or jewel.

Shmekeleh *(SHMEK-a-leh)*—the diminutive of *shmuck*; an inconsequential shmuck; little penis.

Shlepper *(SHLEP-per)*—from the verb *shlep*, to drag. A drip, a jerk; a shabby person; a nonentity who works hard for little compensation; someone who always tags along.

Shlukh *(shlukh)*—a slob, an unkempt person; someone who always has his shirttails hanging out or food on his face.

Shlump *(shloomp)*—a poor dresser; unstylish. Also, someone with bad posture. Like many of these words, can be used as a

Drek!

verb, as when a parent corrects her child's posture with "Don't *shlump*!"

Shtunkener *(SHTUNK-en-er)*—literally, a stinker; commonly, a mean or selfish person.

Shnorrer *(SHNOR-er)*—a beggar, a moocher, a freeloader; someone who wants something for nothing, as in a person who always wants a bite of your sandwich.

Shtinker *(SHTINK-er)*—*shtink* means bad-smelling. A *shtinker* is a bad-smelling person; also a stinker—someone who behaves offensively.

Shikker *(SHICK-er)*—a drunkard; to be drunk. An easy one to remember since *shikker* rhymes with *liquor*.

Shvitzer *(SHVITZ-er)*—literally, someone who sweats; commonly, a braggart; someone who is working up a sweat by trying too hard.

And finally, one *sh* cousin (*shvesterkind*):

Zhlub *(zhlub)*—a slob; a clumsy, graceless person. Jackie Mason says a *zhlub* is a guy who can make a new suit look like a *shmatteh* (or rag).

One can also make up *sh(m)-* words that rhyme with, and thus mock or negate, the words they follow, as in *fame-shmame* (implying that fame is not worth pursuing).

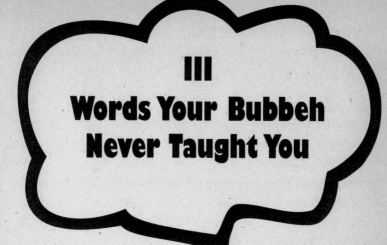

III
Words Your Bubbeh Never Taught You

If you grew up in a typical Yiddish-speaking family you may not have encountered the smutty words and phrases listed below. So who used such language? Well, if your mother ever made reference to an Uncle Artie who was a bum, then Uncle Artie could have been one of the people who used these words. And I'm confident that when Meyer Lansky and Bugsy Siegel argued over who they should kill or extort money from, they spiced up their vocabulary with some of these expressions. Decades ago you would have heard these words on the street corners of the Lower East Side as the young toughs stood under the lampposts smoking their cigarettes. And they would have been used by the street peddlers haggling over whose pushcart bumped whose. Yiddish, like other languages, developed an array of terms to express the raw and the raunchy. First the raw. Here are some beauts that will most assuredly convey your displeasure with someone:

Gay tren zich *(gay TREN zich)*— Go fuck yourself!

Cock zich oys *(COCK zich oys)*— Go take a shit!

Ich cock ahf im *(Ich COCK aff im)*— I shit on him!

Kish mich in tukhes *(KISH mich in TOO-khis)*— Kiss my ass.

Zol es brennen *(zol ess BREN-in)*— To hell with it.

Zolst ligen in drert *(zolst LIG-en in DRERT)*— Drop dead.

Bareh nit *(BAR-eh nit)*— Don't fuck with me.

Drek oif a shpendel *(DREK oyf a SHPEN-del)*—literally, shit on a stick. Used to refer to something worthless.

Er zol einemen a meeseh meshuneh *(er ZOL EIN-eh-men a MEESE-eh meh-SHUN-eh)*— He should go to hell.

Shoyn opgetrent? *(SHOIN OP-geh-trent)*— Are you finished screwing around? Finished fucking?

Khamoyer du ainer *(kha-MOY-er du AIN-er)*— You moron!

Now for the raunchy. Here are words that refer to sex, organs, and homes of ill-repute.

Tukhes lecher *(TOO-khis LEKH-er)*—ass kisser.

Ich hob im in tukhes *(Ich HOB im in TOO-khis)*— I've got him by the ass!

Hinten *(HIN-tin)*—backside, *tuch*, ass, rear end.

Zetz; shtup *(zetz; shtoop)*—literally, a strong punch; commonly, intercourse, fucking.

Tsitskehs *(TSITS-kehs)*—tits.

Baitsim *(BAIT-zim)*—balls.

Lokh *(lawkh)*; **peeric** *(PEE-rik)* or **piregh** *(PEER-egh)*—all these words mean vagina or cunt. *Lokh* also means hole.

Yentz *(yents)*—fuck. Used in the same way as the English word *screw*. "If you don't watch out, he'll *yentz* you."

Yentzer *(YENTS-er)*—fornicator, pimp; also someone who will screw you (in the nonsexual sense).

Nafkeh *(NAF-keh)*; **nekaiveh** *(ne-KAY-veh)*; **kurveh** *(KUR-veh)*—all three mean whore.

Veltz kurveh *(VELTZ KUR-veh)*—the worst kind of whore. *Velt* means world, so a *veltz kurveh* is a woman who fucks anyone and everyone.

Shandhoiz *(SHAND-hoys)*—a house of shame or whorehouse.

Bordel *(BOR-del)*—a bordello, brothel, or whorehouse.

Bayis *(BAY-is)*; **heizel** *(HAYS-el)*—two more words for brothel or whorehouse.

Zoineh *(ZOY-neh)*—a prostitute.

Besuleh *(be-SUL-eh)*—a virgin.

Besulim *(be-SUL-im)*—hymen.

Opgehit *(OP-geh-heat)*—chaste, virginal.

Bristen *(BRIST-en)*—breasts, tits.

Fortz *(fortz)*—fart, pass wind.

Trenen *(TREN-in)*—to rape.

Shlang *(shlong)*—a big penis. Literally, a snake.

Petseleh *(PET-se-leh)*—little penis. Sometimes used affectionately to refer to an infant boy.

Farcockteh *(far-COCK-tah)*—shitty.

Faigeleh *(FAY-ga-leh)*—literally, a little bird; commonly, a homosexual.

Shmuck *(shmuck)*—literally, jewel. The male sex organ; metaphorically, dickhead, idiot, jerk.

Pitsel *(PIT-zel)*—very small, tiny. A little bit of something. Also refers to a penis.

Shvantz *(shvantz)*—another word for penis. Also a dickhead or a man whose behavior is ungentlemanly or obscene.

Momzer *(MOM-zer)*—a bastard, literally and figuratively; a nasty, untrustworthy person.

Meshuggener momzer *(meh-SHOO-gen-er MOM-zer)*—crazy bastard.

Drek *(drek)*—shit. Also used for something cheap, shoddy, or useless.

Tzatske *(TZATZ-keh)*—a toy or an expensive plaything; a bimbo; a mistress.

Tukhes *(TOO-khis)*—buttocks, ass.

Pishen *(PISH-en)*—urinate, piss.

Pisher *(PISH-er)*—a little squirt or little pisser; a nobody. Also used affectionately for a young boy.

Pishakhtz *(PISH-akhtz)*—pee, piss, urine; something worthless or vile.

Bobkes *(BUB-kis)*—literally, goat turds. An absurd idea; an insulting offer, as in "What you're offering me is bobkes."

Groisser potz *(GROY-ser PUTZ)*—big prick. A big idiot.

Tripper *(TRIP-er)*—gonorrhea.

Vemen bares du? *(VAY-men BAR-es DU)*— Who are you kidding? Who do you think you're screwing around with?

Hultie *(HOOL-tee)*—a person of loose sexual morals; a debaucher.

Knipple *(K-NIP-el)*—a hyman. Literally, a knot.

Besulehshaft *(be-SUL-eh-SHAFT)*—virginity.

Pishteppel *(PISH-tep-el)*—pisspot.

Hulyen *(HOOL-yen)*—to carouse, go wild.

IV
Daily Reflections: Bewitched, Bothered, and Besotted (and Other States of Mind)

If Rodgers and Hart (two Jewish boys) had written their love songs in Yiddish instead of English, many a crooner might have found themselves warbling "Farmisht, Fartumelt, and Farblonzhet" instead of the more familiar "Bewitched, Bothered, and Bewildered." (Actually, it's not so outlandish: remember the popular forties song, "Bei Mir Bist Du Shoen," which *is* Yiddish, and means "To me, you're beautiful.")

Yiddish has many words to describe a broad spectrum of psychological states, from excitement and joy to confusion and sorrow. They are graphic, colorful, juicy words, and they are fun to say (like *meshuggeh* for crazy), which may be why so many of them have crept into English usage.

Here are some doozies:

Farblonzhet (*far-BLON-jet*)—lost, hopelessly confused. Describes the person who doesn't know his ass from his elbow, like the kosher butcher who opened a shop in Tokyo.

Fakockt (*fa-KOCKED*)—shitty, badly soiled. Used also when someone is "full of shit."

Drek!

Farfufket *(far-FUF-ket)*—befuddled, taken aback, disoriented, dazed. Overheard in ancient Israel: A *farfufket* sage asked the Lord, "Did I hear you right, God? You want us to cut the tips off our penises?"

Mishegoss *(mih-sheh-GOS)*—usually refers to unreal, impractical, crazy, foolish, or nonsensical thoughts or beliefs; also to clowning around or antic behavior, as in "Stop your *mishegoss*."

Tsedudelt *(tze-DUD-elt)*—wacky, scatterbrained, crazy.

Mosser *(MOO-zer)*—informer; traitor.

Kvell *(kvel)*—to gush with pride; to glow with pleasure; if your child gets a scholarship to Harvard, you can *kvell*. Also, to gloat over an enemy's misfortune.

Makhen a tzimmis *(MAKH-en ah TZIM-ess)*—to make a big deal or a big fuss about something; to blow something out of proportion; make a commotion.

Oysgeputz *(OIS-geh-puts)*—dressed up, overdressed, overly decorated. Refers to someone trying too hard to impress with her clothing: "She's so *oysgeputz*, tsk, tsk."

Nokhes *(NOKH-es)*—to reap joy or happiness.

Sheppen nokhes *(SHEP-en NOKH-es)*—to enjoy enormously; to feel pride (especially from your children).

Yosher *(YOH-sher)*—having sympathy or compassion.

Yoysher *(YOY-sher)*—justice, fairness, integrity.

Shande *(SHAN-deh)*—a shame, an embarrassment.

Tzebrukhen *(tzeh-BROOKH-en)*—broken down. A *tzebrukhener hartz* is a broken heart.

Mekheiyeh *(meh-KHY-eh)*—a pleasure. A good meal is a *mekheiyeh*; so is good sex.

Oysegematert *(OIYS-geh-MOT-airt)*—worn out, weary.

25

Farmatert *(far-MOT-ert)*—exhausted.

Oysgehorevet *(OIS-geh-HOR-eh-vit)*—exhausted.

Oysgemutshet *(OIS-geh-MUTCH-et)*—worked to death, all tired out.

Groisseh fargenigen *(GROY-seh far-gen-EEG-en)*—great pleasure. A date with Demi Moore.

Umglick *(UM-glick)*—a tragedy, a great misfortune; also, an unlucky person. A canceled date with Demi Moore.

Kokhedik *(KOKH-eh-dick)*—excitable; refers to someone "really cooking."

Saikhel *(SAY-khel)*—common sense, good judgment.

Rakhmones *(rakh-MOHN-es)*—pity, compassion.

Koved *(KOH-vid)*—to respect, honor or revere someone.

Oysgedart *(OIS-geh-dart)*—skinny, emaciated, like the models in *Vogue*.

Opgekrokhen *(OP-geh-KROKH-en)*—shoddy, falling apart.

Opgenart *(OP-geh-nart)*—swindled, cheated, fooled, hoodwinked.

Kalamutneh *(kal-a-MUT-neh)*—gloomy, morose, glum.

Mutche *(MOOTCH-eh)*—to struggle along, to eke out a living.

Yontefdik *(YON-tif-dick)*—festive, holidayish, in a party mood.

Fardrost *(far-DROST)*—disappointed.

Kopvaitik *(KOP-vye-tik)*—a headache, a pain in the head, a nuisance.

Krankheit *(KRAHNK-hite)*—sickness. When a poor Jew eats a chicken, one of them has a *krankheit*.

Drek!

After checking his bank statement, Dr. Margolis telephoned Mrs. Rosen.

"The check you gave me came back," he intoned.

"So did my *krankheit*," she replied.

A farshlepteh krank *(a far SHLEPT-eh KRANK)*—a prolonged illness, like doing your income tax returns.

Shtarker kharakter *(sh-TARK-er khar-ARK-ter)*—implacable. Tenacious, stubborn; literally, a strong character.

Shaymevdik *(SHAYM-ev-dick)*—bashful, shy.

Ongeshtopt mit gelt *(ON-geh-shtopt mit GELT)*—literally, stuffed with money; filthy rich.

Ontoisht *(on-TOISHT)*—disappointed.

Foiler *(FOYL-er)*—a lazy man.

Ligner *(LIG-ner)*—a liar.

Khaloshes *(kha-LOSH-is)*—nauseated.

Farglust *(far-GLOOST)*—to yearn or lust for.

Tsedraiter kop *(tzeh-DRAYT-er kop)*—a bungler or someone who is constantly confused.

Tsedrumshke *(tze-DROOMSH-keh)*—befuddled, confused or flustered.

Fartumelt *(far-TOOM-elt)*—bewildered, dizzy, or confused.

Tsemisht *(tse-MISHT)*—confused, befuddled or mixed-up.

Tsetrogen *(tze-TROY-gen)*—absentminded and preoccupied; to have a messy head.

Farmisht *(far-MISHT)*—all mixed-up and confused.

Overheard in a classroom in Brighton Beach:

Teacher: Who can use the word *cultivate* in a sentence?

Farmishter student: I can. When it's forty below in Moscow and the bus isn't coming, it's too *cul ta vait*.

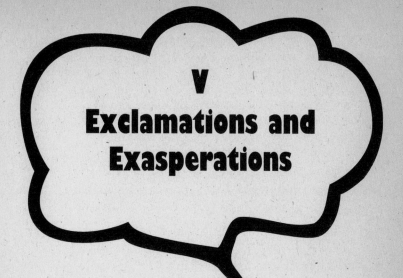

V
Exclamations and Exasperations

Jewish life has always been beset by frustrations and uncertainties. This may explain the abundance of exclamations and exasperations in Yiddish. They range from the poignant to the absurd, from addressing God to chastising some *nudnik* (an annoying, pesty person). And sometimes they are merely a way of letting off steam. Sometimes they imply that life should be better; and sometimes they imply that it couldn't be worse.

Nu *(noo)*—one of the most frequently used words in Yiddish. With a variety of inflections and gestures, it can mean anything from a question (*"Nu?* Did he give you the money?"), to a dare (*"Nu*, show me!") to a simple exclamation (*"Nu!* I told you so"), to an expression of impatience (*"Nu?* So what did he say?").

Nu shoyn *(NOO SHOYN)*— You done yet? Hurry up. Come on and finish up. Aren't you finished?

Oy vay! *(OY VAY)*— How terrible! That's horrible! *Oy vay*, like *nu*, is among the most frequently used expressions in Yiddish.

Beatrice's great-uncle Joseph had a reputation as a *krekhtzer* (complainer), but she agreed to drive him to a family gathering anyway. Soon he began repeating, "*Oy vay*, am I thirsty! *Oy vay*, am I thirsty!" She pulled over and got him a drink, thinking she'd have some peace and quiet for the rest of the way. But as they got back on the highway, she heard from the backseat, "*Oy vay*, was I thirsty! *Oy vay*, was I thirsty!"

Feh! (*feh*)—another popular Yiddish word that can communicate many meanings: That's terrible! I hated that! That stinks! Phooey! How disgusting!

Gevalt (*geh-VALT*)—an exclamation of fear, astonishment, terror. Also, a cry for help. When preceded by *oy* ("Oy gevalt!) it means "That's dreadful!" or "Holy shit!"

A brokh (*ah BROOKH*)— Damn it! This is a curse, a plague. It expresses disgust, misery, or a disaster.

Sally showed her friend her new, very large, diamond ring. "It's the Finklestein diamond," she said. "But it comes with the Finklestein *brokh*."
"What's the Finklestein *brokh*?" her friend inquired.
"Finklestein!"

Gottenyu (*GUTT-in-you*)— Oh, God! Said in despair, anguish, or pity.

Genug iz genug (*geh-NOOG iz geh-NOOG*)— Enough is enough. Stop already. The feeling you get listening to the rock band at your grandson's Bar Mitzvah.

Shveig! (*shvige*)— Shut up! Be quiet!

Gembeh (*GHEM-beh*)— Big mouth!

Hit zich (*HIT zich*)— Look out! Watch it!

Plotz! (*plotz*)—to burst or explode from too much food or excitement, as in "When he told me he loved me I almost *plotzed*!"

Kholileh! *(kho-LEE-leh)*— It should never happen! Don't even think it! God forbid!

Got zol ophiten *(GUTT zol OP-hit-ten)*— God forbid!

Got in himmel *(GUTT in HIM-el)*— God in heaven! An expression of frustration, anguish or fear.

Alevai *(al-eh-VYE)*— It should only happen to me. Please, let it come true.

Zorg zich nit *(ZORG zich NIT)*— Don't worry about it.

> Myron, an octogenarian in an old-age home, was telling his buddy, Jake, that his twenty-six-year-old, sexy attendant had agreed to marry him.
> *"Alevai!"* said Jake. Then, on second thought, he replied, "Don't you know that sex between a man your age and a woman her age can be fatal?"
> *"Zorg zich nit,"* Myron said. "If she dies, she dies."

A klug! A klug tzu mir! *(a KLOOG tzoo MIR)*— Woe! Woe is me!

Makhen a gevalt *(MA-khen a geh-VALT)*—to make a scene; to scream or shout for help.

In miten drinen *(in MIT-en DRIN-en)*—a sudden or unexpected intrusion or interruption.

Koim mit tsores! *(KOIM mit TSOOR-es)*— I barely lived through it; I just made it; I squeaked by.

A shandeh un a kharpeh *(a SHAHND-eh un a KHARP-eh)*— a shame and a disgrace.

Drai zich *(DRAY zich)*— Turn around and keep going. Get moving!

Hert zich ein *(HERT zich eyn)*— Listen to me!

Shoyn genug *(SHOYN geh-NUG)*— That's enough already!

Gib zich a shokel *(GIB zich a SHO-kel)*— Shake a leg; hurry up.

A shreklekheh zakh *(a SHREK-lekh-eh ZAKH)*—a horrible thing!

> A Jewish fellow saw an elderly Jewish gentleman sitting on a park bench, crying. "What's wrong?" he asked.
> "*A shreklekheh zakh,*" the old man replied. "I have a beautiful wife who loves me and satisfies my every sexual desire, and we live in a beautiful house that she keeps like a castle, and she's the best cook in the world."
> "So why are you crying?" the fellow asked.
> "Because I can't remember where I live."

Mish zich nisht arayn *(MISH zich NISHT ar-AYN)*— Don't butt in. Keep your nose out of it.

Gornisht helfen *(GOHR-nisht HELF-en)*— Nothing will help. It's beyond repair, like trying to get a teenage girl off the telephone.

Ti mir eppes *(TEE mir EP-is)*— So, what do you think you can do to me? Nothing!

Varfen an oyg *(VAR-fin on OYG)*—to be on guard, to be vigilant or watchful.

Vart! *(vart)*— Wait! Hold on!

Vos iz? *(VOS IS)*— What's wrong?

Hok nit kein chainik *(HOCK nit kine KHAY-nik)*— Don't talk nonsense. You give me such a headache with your nonsense. Literally, don't bang on the tea kettle.

Nit aheen, nit aher *(nit a-HEEN, nit a-HAIR)*—neither here nor there; *comme ci, comme ça.*

Ti mir nit kein toives *(TEE mir nit KINE TOY-ves)*— Don't do me any favors.

Ahf tzu lokhes *(AHF-tsoo LOKH-es)*— It was fated.

Drek!

Ahf mir gezogt *(ahf MEER geh-ZOKHT)*— It should only happen to me. The only proper response on hearing that someone has won the 10-million-dollar lottery.

Vie shtet geschreiben *(VEE shtet geh-SHRY-ben)*— Who says so? Where does it say that? Literally, where is it written?

A mekheieh *(a meh-KHY-eh)*— Such a pleasure!

Okh un vay *(OKH un VAY)*— Oh, that's terrible! Woe is me!

In drerdt mein gelt *(in DRERDT mine gelt)*— My money went down the drain.

Shoyn vider? *(SHOIN VEED-er)*— What, again?

Az okh un vay *(as OKH un VAY)*— What a misfortune! Tough luck. That's too bad.

Azoy gait es *(a-ZOY gayt es)*— That's how it goes. What can you do?

Azoy? *(a-ZOY)*— Really? No kidding?

Khap nit! *(KHAP nit)*— Not so fast! Don't grab! Take it easy!

Farmakh dos moyl *(far-MAKH dos MOYL)*— Shut your mouth!

Es brent nit *(es BRENT nit)*— Don't get so excited. Calm yourself.

Ich khalesh *(ich KHAL-ish)*— That's too much for me. I'm fainting.

Es vert mir finster far di oygen *(ES vert mir FINST-er FAR dee OY-gen)*— I can't stand any more of it! Literally, it's getting dark before my eyes.

Er krikht vi a vantz *(air KREKHT vee a VANTZ)*— He's a slowpoke. Literally, he's as slow as a bedbug.

Er zitzt oif shpilkes *(air ZITZ oyf SHPIL-kis)*— He's restless, Literally, he's sitting on pins and needles.

Es vet helfen vi a toiten bahnkes *(es vet HELF-in vee a TOYT-en BAHN-kis)*— It's useless. Literally, it'll help like bloodletting on a dead body.

Es past nit *(es PAST nit)*— It isn't proper, it isn't nice.

Groisser gehilleh *(GROYS-eh geh-HILL-eh)*— Big deal! So what!

Got zol ophiten *(GUTT zol OP-hit-ten)*— God forbid.

Ich darf es vi a lock in kop *(ich DARF es vee a LOKH in KOP)*— I need it like a hole in the head.

Loz mich tzu run *(LOZ mich tzu ROON)*— Leave me in peace! Leave me alone!

Me ken tzizetst veren *(meh ken tzi-ZETZT VAIR-en)*— One could burst (in frustration).

Drek!

Me lozt nit leben *(me LUZT nit LAY-ben)*— They don't let you live. People keep aggravating me.

Meshuggeh ahf toit *(meh-SHOOG-eh ahf TOIT)*— Really crazy! Literally, crazy unto death.

Nich du gedakht *(nich DU geh-DAKHT)*— It should never happen to you.

Es hart mich vi di vant *(es HARDT mich vee dee VANT)*— I don't give a damn. Literally, it bothers me like a wall.

Tahkeh a metsiah *(TAK-eh a meh-TSEE-ah)*— A real bargain! Big deal!

Zeit azoy gut *(ZITE a-ZOY GOOT)*— Please, be so good as to . . .

Shlog zich mit Got arum *(SHLOG zich mit GUTT a-ROOM)*— Go fight City Hall. It can't be undone. Literally, go fight with God about it.

Chepeh zich op fun mir *(CHEP-eh zich OP fun meer)*— Get away from me! Leave me alone!

Es iz a shandeh *(es is a SHAHN-deh)*— It's a shame, an embarrassment.

Nisht geferlakht *(NISHT geh-FAIR-lakht)*— No big deal.

Zei nor *(ZYE nor)*— Look here, look at that!

Zei mir frailekh *(ZYE meer FRAY-lekh)*— Be happy!

Zei mir matriakh *(ZYE meer mah-TREE-akh)*— Make an effort. Try.

Zei nit a nar! *(ZYE nit a NAR)*— Don't be a fool.

Zei nit kain golem *(ZYE nit kane GO-lem)*— Don't be stupid. Literally, don't be a zombie.

Zei nit kain vyzoso *(ZYE nit kane vi-ZO-zo)*— Don't be an idiot! Don't be a dickhead.

35

Zeit ahfen ferd *(ZITE AH-fin FERD)*— You're all set. Literally, you're on the horse and ready to go.

Zeit moykhel *(ZITE MOI-khel)*— Excuse me, but . . . Be so good as . . .

Ver volt dos geglaibt? *(VER volt doss geh-GLAYBT)*— Who would believe it?

Vos hart es? *(vos HART es)*— What does it matter? Who cares?

Ain klainechkeit *(ine KLAIN-ekh-kite)*— Big deal! How trivial!

Vos failt im? *(vos FAILT im)*— What's wrong with him? Is he empty-headed?

Vos hert zich? *(vos HAIRT zich)*— What's up? What do you hear?

Vos hert zich epes neies? *(vos HAIRT zich EP-is NY-es)*— What's new? What's happening?

Vos hob ich dos gedarft? *(vos HOB ich DOSS geh-DARFT)*— What do I need that for?

Vos iz mit dir? *(vos IS mit deer)*— What's the matter with you?

Vos kokht zich in teppel? *(vos KOKHT zich in TEP-el)*— What's cooking? What's up?

Vehmen narst du? *(VEH-men NARST du)*— Who are you kidding?

Ver vaist? *(VER VAYST)*— Who knows?

Vos makht dos oys? *(vos makht dos OIS)*— What difference does it make? What does it matter?

Vos nokh? *(VOS NOKH)*— What else?

Farshtaist? *(far-SHTAYST)*— Understand?

Drek!

Fangst shoyn on? *(FONGST shoin ON)*— You're starting up again?

Er bolbet narishkeiten *(er BOL-bet NAR-ish-KITE-en)*— He's talking nonsense.

Er farkockt a kasheh *(er far-COCKT a KASHEH)*— He's turning it into shit. He's making a mess.

Er hot a farshtopten kop *(er HOT a far-SHTOPT-en kop)*— He's thickheaded.

Er hot kadoches *(er HOT ka-DOSH-es)*— He's got nothing. He has nothing but a fever.

Er makht mir a shvartzeh khasseneh *(er makht meer a SHVARTZ-eh KHASS-en-eh)*— He's making a lot of trouble for me. Literally, he's making me a black wedding.

Es gait nit *(es GAYT nit)*— It doesn't work. We don't agree.

Es iz bloteh *(ES is BLOT-eh)*— That's nothing; it's worthless. Literally, it's mud.

Es iz vert a zets in drerd *(es is VERT a ZETS in DRAIRDT)*— It's worthless; it's useless; it's pissing in the wind.

Es vet zich alles oyspressen *(es vet zich AHLL-es OIS-press-en)*— It will all work out. Literally, everything will get ironed out.

Folg mich *(FOLG mich)*— Listen to me; obey me.

Gants goot *(GANTZ goot)*— Very well. It's okay.

Gantseh megilleh *(GANT-zeh meh-GIL-eh)*—a big deal (said sarcastically). Also refers to a long, boring story, speech or event, especially if it is being repeated.

Mir ken im nit puter veren *(mir KEN im nit PUT-er VER-in)*— We can't get rid of him. He won't go away.

Groisseh metsiah *(GROIS-eh meh-STEE-ah)*— Big deal, big bargain.

Gloib mir *(GLOIB meer)*— Believe me!

Ken zein *(KEN ZYNE)*— Could be.

Nokh nisht *(NOKH NISHT)*— Not yet.

Nor Got vaist *(NOR GUTT vaist)*— God only knows.

Makh shnel *(MAKH SHNEL)*— Hurry up!

Nisht gefonfet *(nisht geh-FON-fet)*— Don't fool around; get down to business.

Es shvindelt far di oygen *(es SHVIN-delt far dee OY-gen)*— I'm feeling faint and dizzy.

Lebt a tog *(LAYBT a TOG)*— Enjoy yourself! Have a great time!

Ich bin dich nit mekhaneh *(ich BIN dich NIT meh-KHAN-eh)*— I don't envy you. I wouldn't want to be in your shoes.

Ich hob im feint *(ich HOB im FYNT)*— I hate him.

Ich hob a brireh? *(Ich hob a BREE-reh)*— Do I have a choice? (Meaning, I *don't* have a choice.)

Ich shtarb *(ich SHTARB)*— I'm dying.

> Goldfarb was hit by a car as he crossed the street and was lying on the ground, his life fading quickly. Mrs. Kelly saw the accident and summoned Father Donovan from the nearby church. The priest, not knowing if the man was Catholic, leaned over him and asked, "Do you believe in the Father, the Son, and the Holy Ghost?" Goldfarb opened his eyes in disbelief. *"Ich shtarb,"* he said, "and he's asking me riddles!"

Mein hartz gayt oys *(mine HARTZ gayt oys)*— I'm dying for it.

Es iz ois! *(es is OYS)*— It's over! It's gone!

A nekhtiker tog! *(a NEKH-tik-er TOG)*— It's too late. Forget it.

Drek!

Zol zayn *(zol ZYNE)*— So be it!

Herr nor *(HERR NOR)*— Pay attention! Listen!

Hert zich ein! *(HERT zich EIN)*— Listen up.

Lang leben zolt ir! *(lang LAY-ben ZOLT ihr)*— A long life to you!

Sha! *(sha)*— Be quiet.

A shainem dank in pupik *(a SHAYN-em DANK in POOP-ik)*— Thanks for nothing!

Vos makht es mir oys? *(vos MAKHT es meer OIS)*— Who cares? What difference does it make to me?

Vos iz mit dir? *(vos IS mit DEER)*— What's the matter with you?

Shaymen zolst du zich *(SHAY-men zolst du ZICH)*— You ought to be ashamed of yourself!

Nisht geshtoigen, nisht gefloygen *(NISHT geh-SHTOY-gen, NISHT geh-FLOY-gen)*— What nonsense. Literally, it doesn't stand, it doesn't fly.

Vos makhst du? *(vos MAKHST DOO)*— How are you? How is it going?

Okh un vay! *(OKH un VAY)*— What a misfortune! Tough luck! That's too bad.

Freg nit *(FREG nit)*— Don't ask. You don't want to know how bad it is.

> Sam: *Vos makhst du*, Morris? I haven't seen you in three years.
> Morris: *Freg nit!* In three years I've buried three wives.
> Sam: *Okh un vay!* What happened?
> Morris: Three years ago I married a wealthy widow, but she ate poisoned mushrooms and died. Then two years ago I married an heiress and she ate poisoned mushrooms and died.

39

Then last year I married a successful businesswoman and she died too.

Sam: Poisoned mushrooms again?

Morris: No. A fractured skull. She refused to eat the mushrooms.

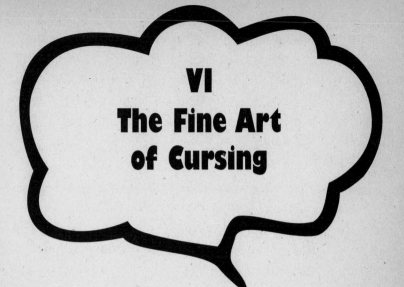

VI
The Fine Art
of Cursing

To curse is to wish for or summon evil on someone. In English, our curses tend to be simple and straightforward, like "Go to hell" or "Drop dead." Yiddish curses can also be direct, as in *Gay in drerd*, meaning "Go die" (literally, "Go in the ground"). But Jews, always a creative people, have applied their inventiveness to elevate cursing to a fine art. Take *Er zol vaksen vi a tzibeleh, mit dem kop in drerd*, which means "You should grow like an onion with your head in the ground"—a succulent curse if ever there was one. Here's a sampling of some good phrases for damning and denouncing:

A kholeria oif dir *(a kho-LAIR-ee-ah OYF deer)*— A plague on you!

Er iz geshtroft *(er is gesh-TROFT)*— He's cursed.

Zolst geshvollen veren vi a barg *(ZOLST geh-SHVOL-en VAIR-in vee a BARG)*— You should swell up like a mountain.

A klug tzu meineh sonim *(a KLUG tzu MINE-eh SON-im)*— A curse on my enemies!

Khamoyer du einer! *(kha-MOY-er du EYE-ner)*— You idiot! You dope! You ass!

Folg mich a gang un gai in drerd *(FOLG mich a GONG un GAY in DRAIRT)*— Do me a favor and drop dead.

A magaifeh zol dich trefen *(a ma-GYE-feh ZOL dich TREF-en)*— A plague should befall you.

A shvartz yor *(a SHVARTZ YOR)*— A black year.

Meineh sonim zolen azoy leben *(MY-neh ZON-em ZOL-en a-ZOY LAY-ben)*— My enemies should live so long!

Zol dir vaksen tzibbeles fun pupik *(zol deer VOX-en TZIB-eh-les fun POOP-ik)*— Onions should grow from your navel.

Zol dich khappen beim boykh *(zol dich KHAP-in byme BOYKH)*— You should only get a stomach cramp.

Zol er tzebrekhen a fus *(zol air tze-BREKH-en a FOOS)*— He should break a leg.

Zol Got mir helfen *(zol GUTT meer HEL-fin)*— May God help me.

Ver derharget *(VAIR der-HAR-get)*— Go kill yourself. Drop dead!

Es dir oys es harts *(es deer OIS es HARTZ)*— Eat your heart out.

A krenk zol im arayn in di yosles *(a KRENK zol im a-RHINE in dee YOS-lis)*— May a disease enter his gums.

Gay bareh di vantsen *(GAY BAR-eh di VANT-zen)*— Go bother the bedbugs.

A ruakh in dein taten's taten arayn *(a RU-akh in dine TAT-ens TAT-en a-RHINE)*— A curse on your father's father.

Der shtikt zolst du veren *(dare SHTIKT zolst du VAIR-en)*— You should choke on it.

Zolst es shtupin in tukhes arayn *(zolst es SHTOOP-en in TOO-khis a-RHINE)*— Shove it up your ass.

Fardray zich dem kop *(far-DRAY zich dem KOP)*— Go screw up your head.

A finsteren sof *(a FIN-ster-en SOF)*— A horrible end should befall you. (May there be) a dark ending for you.

A finsteren yor *(a FIN-ster-en YOR)*— A curse on you. Literally, a dark year.

A finsternish *(a FIN-ster-nish)*— A plague (literally, a darkness) on you.

Geharget zolst du veren *(geh-HAR-get ZOLST du VAIR-in)*— Drop dead. Literally, you should get killed.

Gay feifen ahfen yam *(gay FIFE-en AH-fin YAM)*—literally, go whistle on the ocean; you're wasting your time, you're pissing in the wind.

Gay strashen di gans *(GAY STRA-shin dee GANS)*— You don't scare me. Literally, go scare the geese.

Gay khab enyeh mattereh *(GAY KHAB EN-yeh ma-TER-eh)*— Go to hell.

Gay plotz *(GAY PLOTZ)*— You should explode.

Gay cocken oifen yam *(gay COCK-en OYF-en YAM)*— literally, go shit on the ocean.

Gay fardrai zich dein aigenem kop *(gay far-DRAY zich dine EYE-gen-em KOP)*— Drive yourself crazy, not me. Literally, go twist your own head.

Ich vel dir geben kadoches *(ich VEL deer GEH-ben ka-DOCH-es)*— I'll give you worse than nothing. Literally, I'll give you fever.

Ich hob dich in bod *(ich HOB dich in BOD)*—literally, I have you in the bath. Go drown.

Ich feif oif dir *(ich FIFE oyf deer)*— I despise you. Literally, I whistle on you.

Kein aynhore *(KINE ine-HAR-eh)*—like "knock on wood," meaning keep the evil eye away.

Geb mir nit kein aynhoreh *(geb meer NIT kine ine-HAR-eh)*— Don't give me the evil eye.

Ver dershtikt *(VAIR der-SHTIKT)*— Choke on it!

A gehenem oif im *(a geh-HEN-im OYF IM)*— He should go to hell.

Ver farblonzhet *(VAIR far-BLON-jet)*— Get lost!

Slog zich kop in vant *(SHLOG zich kop in VAHNT)*— Go bang your head against a wall.

Khap a gang *(KHAP a GONG)*— Hit the road, beat it, scram.

Ich hob dich in drerd *(ich HOB dich in DRAIRT)*— Go to hell!

Nem zich a vaneh *(nem zich a VAHN-eh)*— Go jump in the lake. Literally, go take a bath.

Mir velen im bagroben *(meer vel-in IM ba-GROHB-en)*— We'll bury him. We'll do him in.

Er zol vaksen vi a tzibeleh, mit dem kop in drerd *(air zol VACK-sen vee ah TZIB-el-eh, mit dem KOP in DRAIRT)*— You should grow like an onion with your head in the ground.

Miese meshina *(MEESE-eh ma-SHEE-na)*— An ugly ending to you.

45

VII
The Fine Art
of Blessing

Blessings in English, like curses, tend to be direct and unadorned. A forthright "Good luck," "Good health," or "God be with you" is usually sufficient. But Yiddish blessings, like Yiddish curses, are imaginative and colorful—sometimes even poetic. For example, *A gezunt dir in pupik*, doesn't merely wish you good health, it wishes you good health in your *belly*—in your very core. Similarly, *vissen fun tsores*, meaning "You should never know from misery," goes beyond a simple wish for good luck; it entreats that you should never experience bad luck. Having such scrumptious expressions with which to bless your friends and family is, well, a blessing in itself. Here are more:

Fun dein moil tzu Gots oyerin (*fun DINE moyle tzu GUTTS OY-er-in*)— From your mouth to God's ears.

Zolst nisht vissen fun tsores (*ZOLST NISHT VIS-en fun TZOR-es*)— You should never know from human misery, sorrow, or pain.

A leben oif dir *(a LAY-ben oyf deer)*— You should live and be well. Literally, life to you.

Zei gezunt *(zye geh-ZUNT)*— Stay well; stay healthy. Often said when people part.

Mazel tov *(MAH-zel TOV)*— Congratulations! Good luck.

Shmirt zich oys di sheekh *(shmeert zich oys dee SHEEKH)*— Welcome to my house! Literally, wipe your shoes.

Trog es gezunterheit! *(TROG ES geh-ZUNT-er-HITE)*— Wear it in good health.

Zol zein mit glick *(zol ZYNE mit GLICK)*— May you have good luck!

Zorg zich nit *(ZORG zich NIT)*— Don't worry.

A lang leben tzu dir *(a LAHNG LAY-ben tzu DEER)*— A long life to you.

Mir zolen zich bagagenen oif simkhes *(meer ZOL-en zich ba-GAG-en-in oyf SIM-khes)*— May we meet on happy occasions.

A leben oif dein kop *(ah LAY-ben oyf dine KOP)*— A blessing on your head.

Oif mir gezugt *(oyf MEER geh-ZOOGT)*— Let it be said about me.

Zolst nit vissen fun kein shlects *(zolst nit VIS-in fun kine SHLECTS)*— You shouldn't know from anything bad!

Gezundheit *(geh-ZUNT-hite)*— To your health. Said after someone sneezes.

Azoy gezunt *(a-ZOY geh-ZUNT)*— So long as you're healthy.

Got tzu danken *(GUTT tzu DAHNK-en)*— Thank God.

Mrs. Rabinowitz was watching her eight-year-old grandson on the beach near the surf. Suddenly a giant wave engulfed the boy. Mrs. Rabinowitz cried out, "*Got in Himmel*, save

my grandson." Suddenly another giant wave rose up from the sea and tossed the boy back onto the beach, shaken but unharmed. As the relieved grandmother checked her grandson for damage, she exclaimed, "*Got tzu danken*. But, God, he also had a hat."

Zol zein gezunt (*ZOHL ZYNE geh-ZUNT*)— You should be well.

A zein yor oif mir (*a ZYNE yor oyf MEER*)— I should have such good luck. Literally, I should have that kind of year!

Lekhayim (*luh-KHYE-im*)— To life! A toast to your health.

Drek!

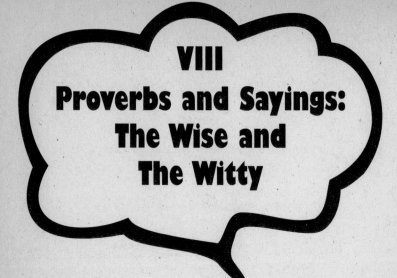

VIII
Proverbs and Sayings:
The Wise and
The Witty

Jews have been around as a community with a continuous identity for thousands of years—probably longer than any other. Certainly long enough to have noticed that people have an almost infinite number of ways of screwing things up: they choose mates for the wrong reason, forget to save for a rainy day, think they can get something for nothing, fail to distinguish between surface and substance, and (perhaps worst of all) fail to learn from their mistakes.

But you don't last thousands of years unless you've also acquired a body of wisdom to pass on from generation to generation. In Jewish culture, some of this wisdom is passed on in formal study, such as the daily Talmud readings by Orthodox Jews. But often it is passed on informally, through proverbs and clever sayings about the state of the human condition that are easy to remember.

A community's proverbs and sayings reveal enduring themes in its character and culture, highlighting what's valued and what's disdained. And, as Ben Franklin and Mark Twain knew (weren't they Jewish?), they help us manage our lives better, providing even the *shmegegees* (jerks) among us with some instant *saikhel* (or good sense).

Other people's problems are never hard to endure. A mackeh unter yenems orem iz nit shver tzu trogen. (ah MACK-eh UNT-er YEH-nems OR-em is NIT SHVAIR tzu TRUG-en)

Nerve succeeds. Chutzpah gilt. (CHUTZ-pah GILT)

A wise man knows what he says, a fool says what he knows. A kluger vaist vos er zogt, a nar zogt vos er vaist. (ah KLUG-er vayst vos er ZOGT, a NAR ZOGT vos er VAYST)

A heavy heart says a lot. A shver hartz redt a sakh. (ah SHVAIR HARTZ rett ah SAKH)

Man plans and God laughs. Menschen makhen planner un Got lakht. (MENTSH-in MAKH-en PLAHN-er oon GUTT LAKHT)

If you have money, people think you are wise, good-looking, and sing well. Az meh hot gelt, iz men klug, schoen, un men ken gut zingen. (az meh HOT gelt, IS men KLUG, SHAYN, oon men KEN goot ZING-in)

Love is sweet; with bread it's better. Di lebeh iz zeez; mit broit iz zi besser. (dee LAY-beh IS zeez; mit BROIT is zee BESS-er)

Petty thieves get hanged; big thieves get pardoned. Klaineh ganavim hengt men; groisseh shenkt men. (KLAIN-eh GAN-a-vim HENGT men; GROISS-eh shenkt men)

Laughter is heard farther than weeping. A gelekhter hert men veiter vi a gevain. (a geh-LEKHT-er HAIRT men VITE-er vee ah geh-VAIN)

When a father gives to his son, both laugh; when a son gives to his father, both cry. Az a tateh shainkt dem zin, lakhen baydeh; az a zin shainkt dem taten, vaynen baydeh. (az ah TAT-eh SHAYNKT dem zeen, LAKH-en BAY-deh; az ah ZEEN SHAYNKT dem TAT-eh, VAYN-en BAY-deh)

Shoemakers go barefoot. Aleh shusters gayen burves. (ah-leh SHUST-ehs GAY-in BOR-ves)

He who understands his foolishness is wise. Der vos farshtait zein narishkeit iz a kluger. (der vos far-SHTAYT ZYNE nar-sih-KITE is ah KLUG-ger)

Wherever you're not seems like a good place to be. Dorten iz gut vi mir seinen nit. (DORT-en IS goot vee meer ZYN-en NIT)

He who has not tasted the bitter cannot know the sweet. Der vos hot nit farzirkht bittereh, vaist nit vos zeez ez. (der vos HOT nit far-ZEERKHT BIT-er-eh VAYST nit vos ZEEZ es)

It's better to die standing up than to live on your knees. Es iz besser tzu shtarben staiendik aider tzu leben oif di kni. (es is BESS-er tzu SHTAR-ben SHTAY-en-dik AY-deh tzu LEB-en oyf di KNEE)

With one rear end you can't sit on two horses. Mit ein hinten zitst men nit oif tsvei ferd. (mit ine HINT-en ZITZT men nit oyf TSVAY FERD)

If you stay at home you won't wear out your boots. Az men zitst in der haim, tsereist men nit kain shtivel. (az men ZITZT in der HAYM, tser-REEST men nit KAYN SHTVEE-vel)

When a thief kisses you, you better count your teeth. Ven a gonif kisht darf men zich di tzein ibertseilen. (ven a GON-if KISHT darf men zich dee TZAYN ib-er-TSAY-lin)

When one must, one can. Az me muz, ken men. (az meh MOOZ, KEN men)

When your enemy falls, don't celebrate, but don't pick him up either. Az der soineh falt, tor men zich nit fraien, ober haibt im nit oif. (az der SON-eh FALT, tor men zich nit FRAY-en, OH-ber HAYBT im nit OYF)

When the stomach is empty, so is the brain. Az der mogen iz laidik iz der moiekh oikh laidik. (az der MOH-gen is LAY-dik, is der MOY-ekh oykh LAY-dik)

When you dig a pit for someone else, you fall in it yourself. Az me grubt a grub far yenem, falt men alain arein. (az me GROBT a GROOB far YEN-em, FALT men ah-LAYN ah-RHINE)

The heart is small and takes in the whole world. Di klainer hartz nemt arum di groisseh velt. (dee KLAYN-eh HARTZ NEMT ah-ROOM dee GROIS-eh velt)

A wise man hears one word and understands two. A kluger far-shtait fun ain vort tsvai. (a KLUG-ger far-SHTAYT fun AYN wort TSVAY)

God looks after fools. Got hit op di naronim. (GUTT heat OOP dee nar-ON-im)

A man should stay alive if only out of curiosity. A mensch zol leben shoin nor fun neigerikeit vegen. (ah MENTSH zol LAY-ben SHOYN nor fun NAY-ger-KITE VAY-gen)

Like parent, like child. Meshugeneh gens, meshugeneh gribbenes. (mes-SHOOG-en-eh GANZ, meh-SHOOG-en-eh GRIB-en-is)

A thief's hat will always burn on his head. Oifen gonif brent dos hittel. (OYF-en GON-if BRENT dohs HIT-el)

The faster, the better. Vos gikher, alts besser. (vos GEE-kher, altz BESS-er)

You don't have to be pretty if you have charm. Me darf nit zayn shayn; me darf hoben khayn. (me DARF nit ZAYN SHAYN; me DARF HOB-en KHAYN)

Don't show a fool something half finished. A nar vaist men nit kain halbeh arbet. (ah nar VAYST nit KAYN HAL-beh AR-bet)

Money goes to money. Gelt gait tzu gelt. (GELT gayt tzu GELT)

That's how the cookie crumbles. Azoy vert dos kikhel tzekrokhen. (ah-ZOY vert dohs KIKH-el tzee-KROKH-en)

One sneezes to the truth. Genosen oifen emess. (geh-NOSS-en OY-fen EM-es)

You can talk and talk and say nothing. Me redt, me redt, un me shushkit zich. (meh RET, meh RET oon meh SHUSH-kit ZIKH)

Everyone has his own craziness. Yeder mensch hot zeiner aigeneh meshugahss. (yeh-der mentsh HOT ZYN-er AY-gen-eh meh-shoo-GAHS)

He's a nitpicker, a troublemaker. Er krekht oyf di gleikheh vent. (ehr KREEKHT oyf dee GLEIKH-eh VENT)

Cheap as borscht. Billik vi vorsht. (BIL-ik VEE borsht)

Pale as a sheet. Blaikh vi di vant. (BLAYKH vee dee VANT)

The money went down the drain. Dos gelt iz tserunen gevoren. (dos GELT is tzeh-RUN-en geh-VOR-en)

Make believe you don't see it. Makh zich nit visindik. (makh zich nit VIS-en-dik)

Talking in vain. Reden tzu der vant. (RED-in tzu dehr VANT)

It's hard to make a living. Es iz shver tzu makhen a leben. (es is SHVAIR tzu MAKH-en a LAY-ben)

He's going in circles. Er drait zich vi a fortz in rossel. (ehr DRAYT zich vee a FORTZ in RUSS-el)

He's got one foot in the grave. Com vos er lebt. (COM vos ehr LAYBT)

He eats like a horse. Er frest vi a ferd. (ehr FREST vee a FERD)

He's ruining it. Er makht a tel fun dem. (ehr makht a TEL fun dem)

He's talking nonsense. Er bolbet narishkeiten. (ehr BOL-bit NAR-ish-KITE-in)

He's turning the world upside down. Er kert iber di velt. (ehr KERT IB-er dee VELT)

Drek!

IX
Food,
Glorious Food

Jews don't just eat. They *fress*! To *ess* is to eat. To *fress* is to eat with relish and fervor. And, as their cardiologists will tell you, Jews eat a lot. If a Jew says he's not hungry, take his temperature. He's probably sick. Indeed, his first thought right after eating is likely to be deciding what he's going to eat later. Food is not merely something to enjoy, but also something to look forward to.

Some Jews eat only kosher food, food that meets various religious imperatives, such as no pork, no shellfish, and only beef and chicken that were slaughtered or processed according to the laws of *Kashrut*. But many Jews follow only some of those restrictions, or follow them only in their homes and not when they eat out. And many don't follow them at all. Want a good Chinese restaurant with great lobster Cantonese and moo shu pork? Don't go to Chinatown; go to an upscale Jewish neighborhood.

It's not that easy to find a strictly Jewish restaurant these days. Not long ago, in the neighborhoods in which Jews lived and worked (which meant large sections of New York City and

Drek!

other urban communities), one didn't have to walk far to find a kosher delicatessen with hot dogs and cold cuts or a dairy restaurant with blintzes, potato pancakes with sour cream, and lox with cream cheese. (The reason for these two distinct kinds of restaurants is because observant Jews don't mix meat and dairy, but do mix fish and dairy.) Even the once-common Jewish bakeries, with their seeded rye and corn breads, *rugalach* pastries and *babka* coffee cakes, are on the wane.

But, just as Yiddish words and phrases have found their way into common everyday usage, so have Jewish foods. Bagels, for example, are everywhere. Mind you, they're not always good bagels, but this staple of Jewish cuisine (with a shmeer of cream cheese, of course) has found its way into every nook and cranny of America, even in places where you won't find any Jews. Nowadays, they even have pizza bagels.

Go to the food court in virtually any shopping mall or to a family restaurant on any main street and you'll find Jewish-style foods on the menu, from kosher hot dogs and pickles, to corned beef and pastrami sandwiches (leave off the melted swiss, please), to matzo-ball soup. And recent news articles report that kosher chickens and other foods have become popular with Americans of all persuasions because of their quality.

Now, all you *fressers* out there, grab your knives and forks and repeat after me:

Ess gezunterhait *(ESS geh-ZUN-teh-HATE)*— Eat in good health.

Khozzer *(KHOZ-er)*—literally, a pig (the animal); also a pig (the person); a gluttonous or insatiable person.

Khozzerye *(khoz-zer-EYE)*—junky food that only pigs would eat; also *junk* food (tasty, but bad for you); also junky things, trash, or crap ("That store has only *khozzerye*").

Bagel *(BAY-gul)*—a roll, hard on the outside, soft in the middle and shaped like a life preserver, which, to some people, it is.

57

Bialy *(bee-YA-lee)*—a disc-shaped roll, thicker around the perimeter and flattened in the middle; typically sprinkled with baked onion bits. Named for Bialystok, a city in Poland, where this roll was created.

Kaiser *(KYE-zer)*—a breakfast roll, light and fluffy on the inside with a thin outer crust (comes with or without seeds).

Kishka *(KISH-kah)*—intestines (from the Russian). Stuffed derma is a sausagelike food made from meat, spices, and flour that is stuffed into a casing made from intestine. To be hit in the *kishkes* is to be clobbered by a penetrating punch to one's midriff.

Blintz *(blintz)*—a pancake folded around cheese, fruit, or potatoes. Like a crepe, but thicker.

Khallah *(KHAL-lah)*—a braided white bread, glazed with egg white. Eaten especially on the Sabbath. Also makes great French toast when sliced thick, dipped in egg, and fried.

Kasha *(KASH-eh)*—a cooked cereal of buckwheat; also served as a side dish with meat.

Kasha varnishkes *(KASH-eh VARN-ish-kes)*—a hearty mixture of buckwheat and broad or bow-tie noodles, sometimes served with meat gravy, sometimes sprinkled with cinnamon and sugar.

Kreplakh *(KREP-lokh)*—a sealed pocket made of dough, which is similar to ravioli and filled with meat or cheese. It is often served in soup.

Shtchav *(tchav)*—sorrel or spinach soup, served cold, especially in hot weather.

Tzimmes *(TZIM-es)*—a side dish made of finely diced vegetables or fruit; also, to make a big commotion over a small thing.

> Leo: Waiter! Waiter!
> Waiter: What is it, sir?

Leo: What is it? Taste this soup!

Waiter: This soup is our house specialty.

Leo: Taste this soup!

Waiter: I've served dozens of bowls tonight and no one's complained.

Leo: That means nothing to me. You taste this soup!

Waiter: All right already. I'll taste it. Where's the spoon?

Leo: AH-HA!

Smetteneh *(SMET-en-eh)*—sour cream.

Holishkes *(HOL-ish-kes)*—cabbage stuffed with a blend of meat and rice and a side of light tomato sauce.

Forshpeiz *(FOR-shpeiz)*—appetizer. Slang: any preliminary activity, including sexual foreplay.

Vurst *(vursht)*—sausage, usually bologna or salami.

Pupiklekh *(POOP-ick-lekh)*—chicken gizzards, eaten plain or in soup.

Gehakteh herring *(geh-HOCT-teh)*—chopped herring.

Gehakteh leber *(geh-HOCT-teh LAY-ber)*—chopped liver.

Shnecken *(SHNECK-en)*—small coffee cakes.

Gribbenes *(GRIB-ben-ess)*—cracklings; chicken skin or fat that is panfried to a crunchy consistency.

Milkhiks *(MIL-khiks)*—any dairy or milk product.

Fleishik *(FLAY-shik)*—any meat product (never mixed with *milkhiks*—it ain't kosher).

Parveh *(PAR-veh)*—food that is neither *milkhidik* (dairy) nor *fleishidik* (meat), but neutral.

Trafe *(trayf)*—nonkosher food or something forbidden.

Tzegaitsich in moyl *(tze-GAY-tzich in MOIL)*— It's so delicious it melts in your mouth.

Rugalach *(RUG-a-luch)*—bite-sized crescent-shaped pastries filled with jam or honey and nuts.

Geshmak *(geh-SHMOCK)*—tasty, extremely delicious, finger-lickin' good.

Mr. Cohen was dying and his son was at his side to comfort him. The old man licked his lips and said, "It smells like your mama is making *rugalach*. They have such a *geshmak*, a little piece on my lips would make me feel so much better." The son hurried to the kitchen, but returned empty-handed.

"So, where is the *rugalach*?" the father inquired.

"Mama said it's for after," his son replied.

A meikhel *(a MY-khel)*—a delicacy or treat.

Taighlekh *(TAYG-lekh)*—little cakes made with honey.

Drek!

Lokshen *(LUCK-shen)*—noodles.

Kugel *(KUG-el)*—a baked pudding made of noodles or potatoes, served by itself or as a side dish. Sometimes sweetened with fruit and raisins.

Lokshen kugel *(LUCK-shen KUG-el)*—noodle pudding.

Lox *(locks)*—smoked salmon, cut into paper-thin slices, often served on a bagel smothered with cream cheese. The unsalted variety is called *nova*.

Hak-flaish *(HOK-flaysh)*—chopped meat.

Boykh vaitik *(BOYKH VAY-tik)*—a stomachache.

Matzo brei *(MAH-tzeh bri)*—a traditional Passover breakfast food of matzo softened in milk or water, mixed with egg and fried with eggs. This dish is then topped with sour cream or sugar, and, more recently, with applesauce.

Borsht *(borsht)*—beet soup served hot or cold, sometimes with a dollop of sour cream.

Knish *(k-nish)*—a dumpling made of potato, meat or kasha. Small knishes are frequently served as appetizers; large ones as a side dish.

Shmaltz *(shmaltz)*—fat drippings; and thus, too sentimental or corny, as in "What a shmaltzy movie!"

Glezel varems *(GLAZE-el VAR-ems)*—a glass of anything warm, like tea.

Boolkes *(BOOL-kis)*—rolls.

Farfel *(FAR-fil)*—noodle dough that has been cut into small, rice-size pieces.

Mir kennen lecken di finger *(meer KEN-en LECK-en dee FIN-ger)*—something that is so delicious, it makes you want to lick your fingers.

Hamentash *(HA-men-tash)*—a pastry, stuffed with prune or poppy seeds, usually eaten at Purim. The name, which means

"Haman's pocket," is derived from Haman, the villain who wanted to murder the Jews in Persia.

Halvah *(HOL-vah)*—a flaky confection made from sesame seeds and honey.

Broit *(broyt)*—bread.

Putter *(POOT-er)*—butter.

Matzo *(MAH-tzah)*—unleavened bread. Matzo balls are dumplings made from matzo meal, floated in chicken soup and most often eaten during Passover.

Latkes *(LAHT-kes)*—grated potato patties fried in oil and usually served with sour cream or applesauce.

Rorzhinkes mit mandlin *(ROR-zhin-kes mit MAND-lin)*—raisins and almonds. The title of a famous Yiddish lullaby.

Mashgiakh *(mach-GEE-akh)*—the inspector of kashrut in kosher food establishments.

And when you are finished eating, you *greps* (GREPZ) or belch.

X
Yiddish for Everyday Occasions

Let's say you go to the Williamsburg section of Brooklyn, New York, for some home-baked Passover matzo, or the Mea She'arim section of Jerusalem to buy a tallis for a Bar Mitzvah boy. In both places you'll find yourself surrounded by people whose primary language is Yiddish. Many will speak English or other languages, but wouldn't it be nice to be able to communicate with them in the *mama loshen*. Whether you're looking for directions, a bargain, or a bathroom, you'll need some everyday words and phrases to make your needs known. Here's a handy collection to get you started:

Hello—*Shah-LOME.* (from Hebrew)

Good-bye—*Ah GOO-tin TAHG.*

Good Sabbath—*Goot SHAB-es.*

Happy Holiday—*Goot YON-tiv.*

I know just a little Yiddish—*Ich KEN nor ah BEE-sel YEE-dish.*

Thanks very much—*ah GROY-sen DAHNK.*

Yes—*Yah.*

No—*Nayn.*

Perhaps—*EF-sheh.*

I don't understand—*Ich far-SHTAY nit.*

My name is _____. *Ich HAYS _____.*

What is your name?—*Vee HAYST ir?*

How much does it cost?—*VEE-fel COST es?*

Too much—*Tzu FEEL.*

It's not good—*Es is NIT GOOT.*

Where is the men's (ladies') room—*Vu is der MEN-eh-TZIM-eh (FROY-en-TZIM-eh).*

I'm hungry (thirsty, sleepy)—*Ich bin HUN-geh-rik (DOR-shtik, SHLEH-feh-rik).*

I am lost—*Ich HOB far-BLON-jet.*

I don't know—*Ich VAYS nit.*

Go away—*GAYT ah-VECK.*

Help!—*Geh-VALT!*

Good morning—*Goot Mor-gen.*

Good evening—*Goo-ten AH-vent.*

How are you?—*Vos MAKHT ir?*

Sit down, please—*ZETZT zich ah-VEK, zayt ah-zoy GOOT.*

I want to go to the airport—*Ich vil TZY-koom-en tzoom FLEE-plahz.*

Please get me a taxi—*ZYTE ah-zoy GOOT, KRIGT mir ah TACK-see.*

North, south, east, west—*TZOR-fen, DOR-em, MIZ-rakh, MEYE-rev.*

Drek!

What street is this?—*VOS-er-eh GAHS iz DOS?*

How much is a ticket?—*VEE-fil COST ah bee-LET?*

Here is my passport—*DORT iz mine PAHS.*

Must I open everything?—*MOOZ ich AHLTS EH-feh-nen?*

What is the flight number?—*VEE iz deer NO-men foon KOORS?*

Can I go by boat?—*KEN ich FOR-in mit a SHIF?*

I am seasick—*Ich bin YAHM-krank.*

What bus do I take?—*VOS-eh AUT-tu-BOOS zol ich NEH-men?*

Where is a gas station?—*VU iz fah-RAHN ah gah-zo-LEEN STANTZ-yeh?*

My car has broken down—*mine AUT-too iz KHAL-ik geh-VOR-en.*

I want to reserve a room—*Ich VIL reh-zehr-VEE-rn ah TZIM-er.*

Excuse me. Be so good as . . . —*zite MOY-khel*

Do me a favor—*TO meer tzu LEEB.*

Not too expensive—*NIT TZU TIE-eh.*

I want a room with a double bed—*Ich VIL ah TZIM-eh MIT ah TOR-plen-bet.*

I do not like this room—*der TZIM-eh geh-FELT meer nit.*

Room service—*bah-DEE-noong in TZIM-eh.*

How much do I owe you?—*VEE-fil KOOMT ich?*

Where is there a good (dairy, kosher) restaurant?—*VU iz dor ah GOOT-eh (MIL-ich-DIK-eh, KOS-heh-reh) restor-RAHNT?*

Waiter!—*KEL-neh!*

Waitress!—*KEL-neh-rin!*

This is overcooked (undercooked)—*dos iz EE-beh-geh-cokht (NIT geh-COKHT).*

I have heartburn—*es BRENT meer OFY-in HARTZ.*

There is a mistake in the bill—*es iz far-RAHN ah TOR-es in KHESH-ben.*

Some Professions

Doctor—*DAWK-teh*

Dentist—*TZOWN-dawk-teh*

Lawyer—*ah-vo-CAHT*

Banker—*bahn-KEER*

Broker—*MEK-leh*

Engineer—*in-zheh-NEER*

Artist—*KINST-ler*

Actor—*ACHT-tor*

Dancer—*TEN-tzeh*

Teacher—*LEH-reh*

Journalist—*joor-nah-LIST*

I want a hammer (pliers, screwdriver, wrench)—*Ich VIL ah HAH-meh (TSVAHNG, SHROY-fin-tzee-eh, MOO teh-dray-eh).*

Where is the nearest bank?—*Vu iz der NOR-ents-teh BONK?*

I have traveler's checks—*Ich HOB REE-zeh-chek-in.*

The business—*dos geh-SHEFT.*

The bill—*der CHESH-bin.*

The company—*dee geh-ZEL-shaft.*

The manager—*der far-VAHL-teh.*

The manufacturer—*der fab-re-KAHNT.*

I want to go shopping—*Ich VIL GAYN EIN-koy-fin.*

Is there an English-speaking person here?—*Iz dor AYE-meh-TZEH vos RET ENG-lish?*

Where is the bakery shop?—*Vu iz dee beh-keh-REH?*

Please bill me—*ZITE ah-zoy GOOT, SHICKT meer ah CHESH-bin.*

Where is the post office?—*VU iz dee POST?*

What time is it?—*VEE-fil HALT deh ZAY-geh?*

XI
Love, Marriage,
and the Jewish Family

If there is anything that has enabled the Jewish people to endure for so many thousands of years, it is the strength of the Jewish family. The overprotectiveness of the Jewish mother has been the subject of countless stories and jokes, and analyses, as has the commitment of the Jewish father to being a good provider for his wife and children. And whether the family atmosphere is calm or contentious, the love for the children is usually lavish and unconditional.

Most Jews can't trace their family tree back more than a few generations, which is understandable, given how often Jews have had to leave their homes and flee for their lives. Yet, in another sense, Jews trace their ancestry back far beyond even the kings and queens of England. The House of Abraham is much, much older than the House of Windsor. Indeed, a recent DNA analysis of Jews from around the world with the name Cohen (or its many variants, such as Kahn, Cohn, and Kahane) supported the notion that most of these Cohens were genetically related and may be the descendants of Aaron, brother of Moses, who was the first *cohen*, which means priest.

The Jewish family has traditionally been an extended family, with aunts, uncles, cousins, and grandparents bound up in (and butting into) each other's lives. Sometimes this sense of family extends in surprising directions. For example, what are the English words for the father or mother of my son- or daughter-in-law? Actually, there are none. But in Yiddish, these words exist, perhaps because in traditional Jewish communities the relationships to one's in-laws were particularly significant.

If you want to know what those words are, read on in this chapter. Along with in-laws words, you'll find words pertaining to families, weddings, love, and romance.

Mishpokheh *(mish-POO-kheh)*—family, clan; people like oneself with whom one feels naturally at home. Sometimes used to refer to one's friends and allies, as in "His whole *mishpokheh* showed up for the meeting."

Yichus *(YIKH-es)*—family lineage. The family tree.

Khupah *(KHU-pah)*—the canopy under which the bride, groom, and rabbi stand during Jewish wedding ceremonies.

Kolleh *(KOL-eh)*—bride.

Khassen *(KHAS-sen)*—bridegroom.

Khasseneh *(KHAS-en-eh)*—wedding.

Khassen-Kolleh *(KHAS-en KOL-eh)*—an engaged couple.

Oys khasseneh *(OIS KHAS-en-eh)*—the marriage is off!

Kalleh moid *(KAL-eh moyd)*—a girl of marriageable age; ripe for marriage.

Kalleh maidl *(KAL-eh MAY-del)*—a young girl not quite eligible for marriage; a preteen.

Kallehniu *(KAL-eh-new)*—little bride.

Goldeneh khasseneh *(GOLD-en-eh KHASS-en-eh)*—fiftieth wedding anniversary.

Oys shiddekh *(OYS SHID-akh)*— The engagement is off.

Hoben khaishek tzu *(hoben KHAY-shick tzu)*—to yearn for.

Gayen tzu kind *(GAY-in tzu KIND)*—about to give birth; go into labor.

Gebentsht mit kinder *(geh-BENSHT mit KIND-er)*—blessed with children.

Nadan *(NAH-den)*—dowry.

Neshumeleh *(neh-SHUM-eh-leh)*—my sweetheart, my darling, my sweet little soul.

Pretzteh *(PRETZ-teh)*—a princess, a prima donna.

Shadchen *(SHAD-khin)*—matchmaker or marriage broker.

> The *shadchen* told Arnie he had a beautiful woman for him to marry. Arnie blustered, "Tell her I'm a good businessman, so before I buy goods, I have to have a sample." The broker relayed the message to the young woman.
> "Tell him I'm also good at business," she replied. "So I don't give samples, but I have lots of references."

Shvengern *(SHVEN-gern)*—to be pregnant.

Es iz a shandeh far di kinder *(es is a SHAN-deh far dee KIND-er)*— It's a shame in front of the children.

Tateniu *(TAT-in-u)*—father, dear. The suffix *niu* is added as an endearment.

Zuninkeh *(ZUN-in-keh)*—dear son, darling son.

Boychick *(BOY-chick)*—little boy.

Bokher *(BOO-kheh)*—a bachelor.

Kaddishel *(KAD-ish-il)*—baby son.

Simkha *(SIM-kha)*—a celebration or a happy occasion.

Yingatsh *(YING-atch)*—a tough, clever boy; a rascal or scamp.

70

Es lost zich essen *(es LOST zich ES-en)*—literally, food that lets itself be eaten. Food that's hard to resist.

Es klempt mir beim hartz *(es KLEMPT meer bym HARTZ)*— It pulls at my heartstrings.

Mein (dos) hartz hot mir gezogt *(mine [dos] HARTZ hot meer geh-ZOGT)*— My heart told me.

Ich hob deer leib *(ich hob deer LEEB)*— I love you.

Es vet zich oyshailen bis der khasseneh *(es vet zich OYS-heilen bis der KHAS-en-eh)*— It will clear up by the wedding.

Hartz vaitik *(HARTZ vay-tik)*—heartache.

Tzebrokheneh hartz *(tze-BROKH-en-eh HARTZ)*—heartbroken.

Khevreh *(KHEV-reh)*—one's group of friends.

Khaver *(KHAV-eh)*—male friend.

Khaverteh *(KHAV-eh-teh)* female friend.

Shaitel *(SHAY-tel)*—wig.

Mohel *(MOY-el)*—the man who performs the ritual circumcision at baby's bris.

Bris *(BRIS)*—the circumcision ceremony.

Terms of Endearment

Kinderlekh *(KIN-der-lekh)*—affectionate term for children; little ones.

Krassavitzeh *(kras-ah-VITZ-eh)*—a beautiful woman.

Zeiskeit *(ZEES-kite)*—sweet thing, sweetie.

Shainkeit *(SHANE-kite)*—a beauty.

Shaineh maidle *(SHAYN-eh MAY-del)*—a pretty girl.

Gezunta Moyd *(geh-ZUNT-eh MOYD)*—a strong, robust girl; a girl with a great body.

Hartzeniu *(HARTZ-en-you)*—my heart's love, my sweetheart.

Tyerinkeh *(TY-er-ink-eh)*—sweetheart, dearest.

Zeiseh neshumeh *(ZEEZ-eh neh-SHUM-eh)*—sweet soul.

Zeiseh raidelekh *(ZEEZ-eh RED-lakh)*—sweet talk.

Basherter *(ba-SHERT-er)*—beloved; fated or destined one.

Gelibteh *(geh-LEEB-teh)*—beloved.

The Yiddish Family Mishpokheh (mish-POO-kheh)

Mameh *(MAH-meh)*—mother.

Tateh *(TAH-teh)*—father.

Vibe *(vibe)*—wife.

Mann *(mahn)*—husband.

Tokhter *(TOKH-ter)*—daughter.

Zin *(ZIN)*—son.

Shvester *(SHVEST-er)*—sister.

Bruder *(BROOD-er)*—brother.

Tante *(TAN-teh)* or **memmeh** *(MEE-meh)*—aunt.

Fetter *(FET-er)* or **oncle**—uncle.

Plemenitze *(pleh-MEN-it-zeh)*—niece.

Plemenik *(pleh-MEN-ick)*—nephew.

Cuzin (masc. *koo-ZEEN*; fem. *koo-ZEEN-eh*)—cousin.

Bubbeh *(BUB-beh)*—grandmother.

Zaide *(ZAY-deh)*—grandfather.

Aynekel *(AYN-ek-el)*—grandchild.

Ayneklekh *(AYN-ek-lekh)*—grandchildren.

Elter bubbeh *(EL-teh BOO-beh)*—great-grandmother.

Elter zaide *(EL-teh ZAY-deh)*—great-grandfather.

Ur-aynekel *(oor-AYN-ek-el)*—great-grandchild.

Ur-ayneklekh *(oor-AYN-ek-lekh)*—great-grandchildren.

Mizinikil *(miz-IN-ik-il)*—the last child in the family.

The Yiddish Family-by-Marriage

Makhahtanim *(makh-ah-TAH-nim)*—in-laws.

Shviger *(SHVAY-ger)*—mother-in-law.

Shver *(shver)*—father-in-law.

Shvegerin *(SHVEH-geh-rin)*—sister-in-law.

Shvoger *(SHVOG-er)*—brother-in-law.

Shneer *(shneer)*—daughter-in-law.

Aidem *(AID-im)*—son-in-law.

Get *(get)*—a divorce.

Drek!

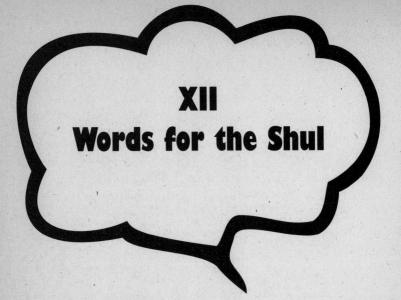

XII
Words for the Shul

The shul or synagogue is, of course, not the place for slang or dirty words. It is a place for prayer, reverence, and celebration. It is where one learns how to live a good life day by day and where the milestones of life are blessed through ceremony and ritual. It is where, despite hardship and pain, the community comes together to be reminded of, and give thanks for, the blessings that God has bestowed.

Brokheh *(BROKH-eh)*—a blessing; a prayer of thanksgiving and praise.

Shammes *(SHAH-mis)*—the official or sexton whose main duty is to take care of the synagogue.

Mikva *(MIK-vah)*—indoor bath or pool for ritual purification, particularly during and after menstruation. A bride-to-be always goes to the mikva before her wedding.

Menorah *(men-OR-eh)*—a candelabra lit on Chanukah.

Haggadah *(ha-GAD-eh)*—the book containing the story of the Exodus, used at the Seder service on Passover.

Reb *(reb)*—rabbi; a title of respect for a religious scholar.

Shabbos *(SHA-boss)*—the Sabbath.

It was a beautiful Shabbos morning and the rabbi, pretending to be sick, snuck out to the golf course instead of conducting the service. Moses in heaven reported the rabbi's deception to God, who sent a strong wind in the rabbi's direction as he teed off on the difficult fourth hole. The ball soared and landed directly in the hole. Moses was perturbed. "God, the rabbi is not fulfilling his responsibilities to his congregation and you give him a hole in one. You call this a punishment?"

"Sure," replied God. "Who can he tell?"

Rebitsin *(REB-it-zin)*—the rabbi's wife. Sometimes said sarcastically to refer to a haughty or pretentious woman ("Oh, she thinks she's the Rebitsin!").

Shiva *(SHI-va)*—seven-day mourning period for the deceased.

Pushke *(PUSH-keh)*—a coin box for charity.

Tallis *(TAL-is)*—prayer shawl (used by men only).

Tefillin *(T'FILL-in)*—phylacteries: leather boxes on straps that are wrapped around the left arm and forehead, which contain parchments with passages from the Torah. They are worn by males over thirteen years of age during prayer.

Davenen *(DAV-in-in)*—praying.

Davenen minkheh *(DA-vin-en MINKH-eh)*—reciting the afternoon prayer.

Sidder *(SID-er)*—book of daily prayers.

Kaddish *(KAD-ish)*—a prayer of mourning that praises God.

Talmud *(TAHL-mud)*—the book of commentary on, and interpretation of, Jewish law as it is given in the Torah.

Tashlikh *(TASH-likh)*—ceremony on Rosh Hashanah, the Jewish New Year, in which crumbs of bread symbolizing one's sins are thrown into water.

Bentschen lekht *(BEN-shon lekht)*—to recite prayers over lit candles.

Bas Mitzvah *(BAS MITZ-vah)*—a girl who has come of age in the religious sense. Also has come to refer to the ceremony and celebration of this event.

Bar Mitzvah *(BAT-MITZ-vah)*—a boy who has come of age in the religious sense. Also has come to refer to the ceremony and celebration to mark the occasion.

Kaftan *(KAF-ton)*—the long coat worn by religious Jews.

Bal Torah *(BAL TOR-ah)*—a learned man, a scholar of the Torah.

Yortseit *(YOUR-tzite)*—the annual commemoration of the death of parents or other relatives.

Neshumeh *(neh-SHUM-eh)*—a person's soul or spirit.

Opgehitener *(OP-geh-HEET-en-eh)*—a pious person.

Benchen *(BENCH)*—saying a blessing.

Shalakh mohnes *(SHA-lakh MOY-nes)*—purim goodies.

Shokhet *(SHO-khet)*—ritual slaughterer of animals.

Leveiyeh *(le-VIE-eh)*—funeral.

Khazen *(KHA-zin)*—a cantor who sings prayers in a synagogue.

Yizkor *(YIZ-keh)*—memorial service for the dead.

Minyan *(MIN-yen)*—the quorum of ten men required in Jewish law to hold religious services.

Mizrakh *(MIZ-rakh)*—the front row in the synagogue set aside for esteemed members of the congregation. Literally, east.

Yarmelkeh *(YAR-mel-keh)*—skullcap worn by observant Jewish men.

Dybbuk *(DIB-ik)*—an evil spirit, condemned to wander the earth because of past sins, that takes possession of living persons and makes them mad.

Mogen Dovid *(MO-gen DOV-id)*—the Star of David; the six-pointed Jewish star that is the national symbol of Israel.

Yeneh velt *(YEN-eh velt)*—the next world; the hereafter.

Malekh-hamovess *(MAL-ekh hom-OV-es)*—the angel of death.

Malekh-hamovesteh *(MAL-ekh hom-ov-ES-teh)*—the female angel of death. Sometimes used to describe a bad wife.

Mezuzah *(me-ZOO-zah)*—a small box containing a section of Deuteronomy placed on the right door frame of entrances.

Tzaddik *(TZAD-ik)*—a pious and righteous person.

Yeshiva bokher *(yeh-SHEE-veh bokh-er)*—a student of religion.

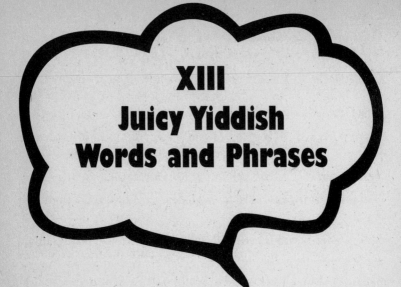

XIII
Juicy Yiddish
Words and Phrases

Even those who know only a little Yiddish will probably have felt the temptation to insert a Yiddish word or phrase into their normal English conversations, either because the Yiddish term is more precise or more amusing than any English word they can think of.

For example upon seeing a cute child, one might exclaim, "What a *punem*!" *Punem* means face, but somehow, "What a face" doesn't convey quite as evocatively the deliciousness of that cute little face.

Or one might say, "Now this, *takeh*, is a noodle pudding." Inserting *takeh* this way conveys that this noodle pudding is not merely great noodle pudding, it is the essence of great noodle puddings. It could even mean that in a lifelong search for the greatest noodle pudding, one has finally found a candidate. It's hard to give an exact definition of *takeh*. The words "really," "certainly," and "of course" are close, but none captures all the connotations. And *takeh* can be applied to virtually anything. (For example, "This, *takeh*, is a pair of shoes," conveys that the shoes are everything shoes should be: comfortable, beautiful, durable, you name it.)

Below are many more examples of such juicy Yiddish words and phrases that one might come across or use in everyday English conversation.

Kitsl *(KITZ-el)*—tickle.

Farfoylt *(far-FOLT)*—rotten, decayed.

Handl *(HOND-le)*—to bargain.

> As one story tells it, Moses came down from the mountain clutching the tablets and said to the Israelites:
> "I did a little *handling* and got him down to ten. Unfortunately, Adultery is still one of them."

Fartrasket *(far-TRAS-ket)*—ornate, decorated or embellished.

Fardart *(far-DART)*—skinny, dried-out.

Kuntzen *(koontz-in)*—tricks, stunts, pranks.

Ongevorfen *(ON-geh-vor-fin)*—cluttered-up, littered, messy.

Tsores *(TZOR-es)*—worries, troubles, woes.

> Grossman got a call from his doctor with the results of his blood test. "Grossman, we've got *tsores*. I've got bad news and worse news," said the doctor. "The bad news is you have only twenty-four hours to live."
> "Oh, no," said Grossman. "What could be worse news than that?"
> "I've been trying to reach you since yesterday."

Ahf tsores *(of TZU-ress)*—to be worried or in trouble.

Geharget *(ge-HAR-get)*—killed, slain, or as a mobster would put it, "whacked."

Tahkeh *(TAHK-eh)*—Really! Certainly!

Untershmeikhlen *(OON-ter-SHMYEKH-len)*—to butter up.

Vortspiel *(VORT-spiel)*—pun; a play on words.

Simcha *(SIM-cha)*—a joy or a joyous occasion, like marrying off your last daughter.

Bubbeh meisseh *(BUB-eh MY-seh)*—literally, a grandmother's story; an old wives' tale; a nonsensical belief.

Tokhes oifin tish *(TOO-khis oyf-en TISH)*—literally, put your ass on the table. Let's get down to business. Put up or shut up.

Farfalen *(far-FAL-in)*—lost.

Shvakhkeit *(SHVAKH-kite)*—weakness.

Billik vi borsht *(bill-EK vee BORSHT)*—as cheap as borsht. A bargain.

Tzu kumen oifen zinen *(tzu KUM-in OYF-en ZIN-en)*—to enter one's thoughts or come to mind.

Mitzvah *(MITS-veh)*—a good deed.

Fardenin a mitzveh *(far-DEEN-in a MITZ-veh)*—to earn a blessing by doing a good deed.

A lek un a shmek *(a LEK un a SHMEK)*—refers to anything done inadequately, carelessly, too quickly. Literally, a lick and a sniff.

Abi tzu zein mit dir *(a-BEE tzu ZYNE mit deer)*—as long as I can be with you.

An ain un aintsikeh *(on AYNE un AYNE-tze-keh)*—the one and only.

Makhen a tzimmis *(MAKH-en ah TZIM-is)*—to make a big deal about a small thing. To blow something out of proportion.

Spilkes *(SHPIL-kes)*—needles and pins. Also refers to someone who is "sitting on needles and pins" or is impatient or in a hurry.

Nuch a mol *(NUCH a mul)*—one more time; what, again?

Drek!

When Izzy came back from the doctor he passed on to his wife the sad news that he had less than twelve hours to live. Grief-stricken, Sarah told him she wanted to make love to him the way they had when they were young lovers. When they were finished, Izzy, still filled with passion, asked if they could do it again. His loving wife complied. After another long bout of lovemaking, Izzy snuggled up to Sarah and said, "*Nuch a mol.*" "That's easy for you to say," retorted Sarah. "You don't have to get up in the morning."

Geferlekh *(geh-FAIR-lekh)*—awful.

Eingeshpahrt *(EIN-geh-SHPART)*—stubborn.

Khmalyeh *(KHMAL-yeh)*—a punch, bang or slam.

Khropen *(KHROP-in)*—to snore.

Fonfen *(FON-fin)*—to snore.

Gekhropet *(geh-KHROP-et)*—snored.

Shmutz *(SHMOOTZ)*—dirt, filth.

Emmes *(EM-is)*—the truth. Absolutely. Definitely.

Gatkes *(GAHT-kes)*—long johns; warm underwear.

Sitzfleish *(ZITZ-flaysh)*—patience; concentration.

Yenems *(YEN-ems)*—someone else's; belonging to other people.

Gleikhvertel *(GLEIKH-vert-el)*—pithy saying, wisecrack, pun or proverb.

Kuntzen *(KOONTZ-in)*—tricks, stunts, pranks.

Di emmeseh shoyreh *(dee EM-es-eh SHOY-reh)*—the real McCoy; the genuine article.

Lapeh *(LAP-eh)*—a slap. Literally, a big hand.

Gestank *(geh-SHTAHNK)*—a bad odor, a stink.

Pupek *(POOP-ik)*—belly button, navel.

Dingen *(DING-in)*—to bargain, hire or rent.

Nisht geferlekh *(NISHT geh-FAIR-lekh)*—not bad. No big deal.

Aroyze gevorfen gelt *(ah-ROYZE geh-VOR-fin GELT)*—money wasted.

Klappen oif der vant *(KLAP-in oif der VANT)*—literally, to bang on the wall. Asking your cheap landlord to paint.

Mezumeh *(meh-ZUME-eh)*—ready cash.

Khokhmeh *(KHOKH-meh)*—a wise saying; knowledge or wisdom.

Goldeneh medineh *(GOLD-en-eh meh-DEEN-eh)*—the United States. Literally, a golden country.

Efsher *(EF-sher)*—maybe.

Oremkeit *(OR-em-kite)*—poverty.

Tei mir a toiveh *(tee meer a TOY-veh)*—do me a favor and . . .

Tzum glick, tzum shlimazel *(tzum GLICK, TZUM shli-MAZ-el)*—for better and for worse.

Es tut mir bahnge *(es TOOT mir BAHNG)*—I'm sorry. I regret it.

Es is shver tzu makhen a leben *(es is SHVAR tzu MAKH-in a LAY-bin)*— It's hard to make a living. It's hard to make ends meet.

Braiter vi lainger *(BRAY-ter vee LANE-ger)*—happy, ecstatic.

Shmeikel *(SHMYE-kel)*—to deceive, trick or con.

Shushkin zich *(SHUSH-kin zich)*—to talk behind someone's back; to gossip.

Mazel *(MAZ-el)*—Luck. That which only a competitor possesses.

Shtik mazel *(SHTIK MAZ-el)*—a bit of luck.

Groisser fardiner *(GROY-ser far DEEN-er)*—some bread-winner!

Me lost nit leben *(meh LOST nit LAY-ben)*—they don't let you live.

Shmeikel *(SHMI-kel)*—swindle, trick.

Hetskentzich *(HETS-ken-zich)*—to dance with joy.

Farpotchket *(far-POTCH-ket)*—messy or overdone. You can *farpotchkeh* (the verb) almost anything, from clothes to your artwork ("The painting was good, but then you go and *farpotchkeh* it").

Tumel *(TOO-mel)*—confusion, noise, uproar.

Khoyzik makhen *(KHOI-sik MAKH-en)*—to make fun of; to ridicule.

A deigeh hob ich *(ah DAY-geh hob ich)*— I should worry; I don't care.

A dank *(ah DANK)*— *Thanks.*

> The tailor said it would take two weeks to make pants for Mr. Frank, but they weren't ready until six weeks later.
>
> "How come," asked Mr. Frank, "God was able to create the whole world in six days, but it took you six weeks to make just one pair of pants."
>
> "You got a *metsieh*," replied the tailor as he held up the pants. "Look at the condition of the world—and look at this gorgeous pair of pants."

A metsieh fun a gonif *(ah me-TZI-eh fun a GON-if)*— It's a steal.

A nekhtiker tog *(a NEKH-tek-er TOG)*—finished. Gone. Impossible.

A shaineh, raineh, kaporeh *(a SHAYN, RAYNE kap-OR-eh)*— It serves him right. He deserved it.

Langeh dronitzeh *(LANG-eh DRON-its-eh)*—a long, thin girl.

Antoisht *(an-TOYSHT)*—disappointed.

Unterkoifen *(UN-ter KOY-fin)*—to bribe.

An alteh makhsaifeh *(an ALTEH makh-SAYF-eh)*—an old witch.

Mordeven zich *(MOR-deh-vin ZICH)*—to work hard.

Kibbitz *(KIB-itz)*—to joke or kid around; to wisecrack or tease.

Parnosseh *(par-NOS-eh)*—livelihood.

Aroysgevorfeneh gelt *(ah-ROYCE-geh-VOR-fin-eh GELT)*— wasted money; money thrown away.

Arumgevolgert *(ah-ROOM-geh-VOL-gert)*—loafed, wandered around.

Baroygis *(bar-OY-gis)*—angry.

Shvindel *(SHVIN-del)*—a swindle, a fraud.

Billik *(BIL-ik)*—cheap.

Bashert *(bah-SHAIRT)*—it's written, fated.

Shmeer *(shmeer)*—literally, to grease lightly. One can *shmeer* a bagel with cream cheese, a palm with money (meaning to bribe) or a person with compliments (meaning to flatter).

Shmatteh *(SHMAH-teh)*—a rag; anything useless. Can be used to wipe up a *shmeer*.

Vaitik *(VAY-tik)*—an ache or pain.

Frassk *(frahsk)*—a hard slap with the back of the hand.

Nudjen *(NOOD-jen)*—to pester or nag.

Shmuesen *(SHMOO-sen)*—to chat, to shmooze.

Gedult *(geh-DULT)*—patience, stamina. What you need when your kids become teenagers.

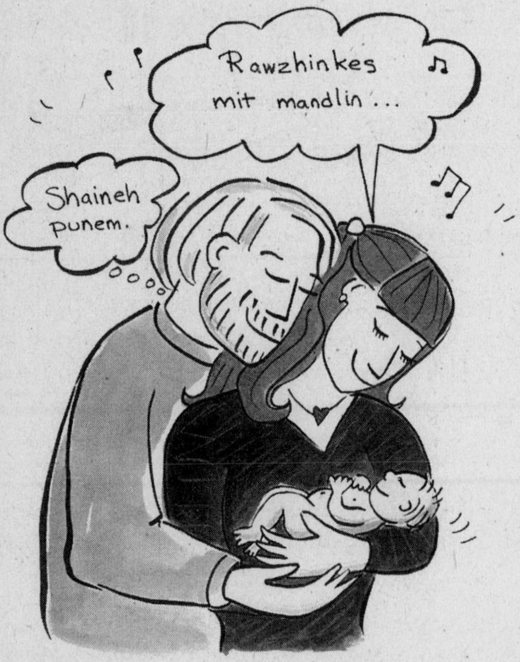
Rawzhinkes mit mandlin . . .
Shaineh punem.

XIV
Yinglish: The Yiddish You Already Know Without Knowing It

Jews have played a central role in American culture for over a century, making major contributions to literature, theatre, film, music, the social and physical sciences, comedy (in vaudeville, on radio, and on television), as well as to business, industry, and the law. While many Jewish leaders worry about Jews assimilating into the dominant culture, in many instances the opposite has occurred, with the dominant culture embracing and adopting Jewish words and ways. The term *Yinglish* has been used to refer to the many Yiddish words and expressions that have become common in English, used by Jews and non-Jews alike.

Yinglish includes such widely used Yiddish words as *chutzpah* and *gonif*, as well as such basic Yiddish locutions as *fancy-shmancy*, *All right already!*, and *Good-looking, he's not*. Here are some more examples of Yinglish terms that I'm sure you will recognize:

Mishmash (*MISH-mash*)—a mess, a hodgepodge, a jumble, like a child's finger painting or, for some people, a canvas by Jackson Pollock.

Potchkeh *(POTCH-keh)*—to fuss with or mess up. When you *potchkeh*, you end up making a *mishmash*.

Nudge *(NOODGE)*—an annoying person.

Shmooze *(SHMOOZ)*—a friendly, leisurely chat. To befriend.

Bohmerkeh *(BUM-erk-eh)*—a female bum or tramp.

Gunzel *(GON-zel)*—a drifter or bum. Also, a novice thief or gangster.

Fressing *(FRESS-ing)*—to enjoy good food and drink—and lots of it. Also, to pig out.

Shlock joint *(SHLOCK joint)*—a store that sells cheap, low-grade merchandise, or secondhand or cut-rate goods, where bargaining over prices is expected.

Shmaltzy *(SHMALTZ-ee)*—sentimental and corny—probably derived from *shmaltz*, the Yiddish word for fat.

Handl *(HON-dle)*—to bargain or try to make a deal.

Tough tukhes *(tough TOO-khis)*—literally, tough ass. Tough luck, too bad; you better learn to live with it.

Shmo *(shmoh)*—a jerk, a fall guy; someone of whom one can easily take advantage.

Yenta *(YEN-teh)*—a gossipy woman.

Shtik *(SHTICK)*—a piece, bit, a lump of something. Also a bit of acting, like a skit, but usually referring to comedy or slapstick.

Icky *(ICK-ee)*—something nauseatingly unpleasant; sticky, gooey or over-sweet.

Shlep *(SHLEP)*—to drag around.

Shnook *(shnook)*—a sad sack, a meek person.

Drek!

Here are some English phrases whose meaning or syntax is borrowed from Yiddish.

Do me something.
Again with . . . (your nagging!).
Be well.
Boo-boo.
Don't ask.
Eat a little something.
Bite your tongue.
Enjoy!
Enough already.
Big deal!
Get lost!
Wear it in good health.
How's it going?
What is, is; what was, was.
Better you should . . .
All right already.
What's to lose?
He's a big nothing.
Could be.
What's with (Sammy)?
Don't ask.
Who knows?
Who needs it?
Cockamamie.
You should excuse the expression . . .
You want to hear something?
That's what *you* say.
Go talk to a wall.
A nice thank you!
Drop dead!
That's all I need.
That's for sure.

I should worry.
It can't hurt.
By me it's . . .
It shouldn't happen to a dog.
Likewise, I'm sure.
Listen up.
How's by you?
So who's watching the store?

Afterword: What Yiddish Looks Like, Reads Like, and Morphs Like

Open a Spanish, French, or German book and you can read it, even if you don't know what the words mean (although you'll mispronounce many of them). Open a Yiddish book and you won't be able to read a thing because Yiddish uses the Hebrew alphabet, not the Roman alphabet used in English and most other European languages. What's more, you will probably open the Yiddish book at the wrong end, since Yiddish reads from right to left (that is, Yiddish books begin on what in English would be the last page; and the first word on a Yiddish line would be the last word on a line of English text).

In this chapter I'll provide a very brief survey of some aspects of Yiddish as a written and spoken language. You'll learn a bit about its grammar or morphology, such as how plurals and some basic tenses are formed, its division into masculine and feminine endings, and a few other structural patterns.

Making Plurals

The way one makes plurals in Yiddish could not have been devised by someone with a *Yiddisher kop*. It is incredibly complicated. In fact, there are no less than seven major ways of turning a singular noun like mother (*mameh*), child (*kihnd*), bed (*bet*), house (*hoyz*), or book (*bukh*) into a plural.

With some words you add an *es* sound; for example, *mameh* becomes *mamehs*. Other words get an *er* sound; for example, *kihnd* becomes *kihnder*. Still other words add an *en* sound; for example, *bet* becomes *betten*. To make things even more complicated, for many words that get the *er* ending, the preceding vowel also gets converted to a different sound. For example, *hoyz* becomes *hyzer* and *bukh* becomes *bikher*. But that's not all. Some words don't get a special ending at all; only a vowel changes. For example, *tog* (day) becomes *tayg* (days). And to add to the confusion, many nouns don't change at all in the plural; only the preceding article changes. For example, *der messer* (the knife) becomes *di* [dee] *messer* (the knives).

How do you know which words take which endings and what the vowel changes are? Well, there doesn't appear to be any logical rule. You just have to learn it.

Oh, there's one more thing. Yiddish words that are taken from Hebrew are pluralized as in Hebrew, by adding *im* [eem]. So, *kibbutz* becomes *kibbutzim*, *mamzer* (bastard) becomes *mamzerim* (a bunch of bastards), and *badkhen* (a jokester or gag-maker) becomes *badkhenim* (a gaggle of gagsters).

Talking About the Past and the Future

Let's start with the word *study*, which is something that all Jews, being "people of the book," are supposed to do a lot of.

Drek!

The Yiddish for "I study" and "I am studying" is *Ich lern*. The Yiddish for "I studied" or "I have studied" is *Ich hob gehlernt* [hard g]. So, from present tense to past, three things changed: the auxiliary verb *hob* (meaning "have") was added. *Geh* became the first syllable of the verb. And the last sound of the verb became a *t*.

These three transformations are common to many Yiddish verbs as they change from the present tense to the past, although often the last sound changes to *en* instead of a *t*, as when *Ich zing* (I sing) becomes *Ich hob gehzingen* (I sang). But there are some verbs that don't get the prefix *geh*, as when *Ich bashaf* (I create) becomes *Ich hob bashafen* (I created). Also, the auxiliary verb *hob* goes through its own set of changes to conform to the pronoun—for example, if the studier is "you," "he," or "we," one would say *Du host* [hahst] *gehlernt*, *Er hot gehlernt*, or *Mir hoben* [hahben] *gehlernt*.

Happily, it's easier in Yiddish to talk about the future than the past—grammatically speaking, that is. All you have to do is add the auxiliary verb for *shall* or *will* to the infinitive. So "I shall study" becomes *Ich vel lernen*; "You will study" becomes *Du vest lernen*; and "We will study" becomes *Mir vellen lernen*.

Masculine/Feminine

In Yiddish, words are generally feminized by the addition of *eh*, or a consonant such as *t* or *k* followed by *eh* (*teh, keh*). The masculine form sometimes gets an *er* [ehr] ending and sometimes no special ending at all. For example, the noun *balehbos* (which means the man of the house, the manager, or the boss) is already in masculine form, but the feminine form, *balehbusteh* (referring to an expert homemaker or housekeeper or the wife of the manager or boss), adds the *teh* ending. When the adjective *fartootst* (which means bewildered or confused) refers to a man, it becomes *A fartootster*, while a woman is *A fartootsteh*. As another example, the verb *kvetch* (meaning to

95

complain or gripe) changes to *kvetcher* when it refers to a man and to *kvetcherkenh* when the complainer is a woman.

The Suffix -ish

A common way to convert a verb into a noun is by adding -*ish* to the word. So when *einredin*, which means to convince oneself of something not true, becomes *einrednish* it refers to a delusion. Similarly, when *balbata* (to be quiet) becomes *balbatish* it means quiet, respectable, well-mannered.

The Suffix -keit

In Yiddish, adding the suffice -*keit* to the end of a word is equivalent to adding "ness" in English.

edel (gentle)—**edelkeit** (gentleness)
yiddish (Jewish)—**yiddishkeit** (Jewishness)
narish (foolish)—**narishkeit** (foolishness)

The Suffix -nik

When -*nik* is added to the end of a word it denotes a devotion or commitment to some cause or belief. So a *peacenik* is someone devoted to peace. Sometimes -*nik* has a derogatory connotation, implying the person is a fanatic, cultist, or faddist. As the following examples show, this ending has become quite common in English usage.

No-goodnik
Beatnik

Drek!

Peacenik
Refusenik
Sicknik
Nudnik
An animal-**rightsnik**

Diminutives

Diminutives are often used as endearments, as when a child is called a *bubbeleh* or "little grandmother." The diminutive is commonly formed by adding an *leh* to a final vowel; it is also formed by adding an *hel* to a final consonant.

Tatah—tatatleh (father—little father)

Mameh—mamehleh (mother—little mother)

Tsatskeh—tsatskeleh (toy—little toy; often used to refer to a woman who is a plaything or bimbo)

Yingeh—yingaleh (youth—little boy)

Nebekh—nebekhel (a nothing—a little nothing)